SOUTH CENTRAL L.A. CHRONICLES:
DIVINE
INTERVENTION

COREY HALL

ISBN: 979-8-9911653-0-3 (Paperback)
ISBN: 979-8-9911653-1-0 (eBook)

Library of Congress Control Number: 2024914936

Editor: Frank D. Williams, Killing It Write
Cover Design: Juan Roberts, Creative Lunacy
            Sharief Morrow, pureskillart@gmail.com
Book Publishing Coach: Willa Robinson

DISCLAIMER:
This memoir was written without names: only people, places, and things.

Take a ride with me through South Central L.A., I can show you better than I can tell you!

These chronicles were written from primary and secondary experiences. This memoir will inspire, move you, and provide healing to the core.

Warning: Graphic content

Published by:

Pen Cry Publishing
Los Angeles, California
hallcorey.com

Printed in the United States of America

DEDICATION

I dedicate the first third of this book to my pops, Tim Hall. There was almost nothing he could not do; he made all things possible. I saw it with my own eyes. I miss his jokes, him singing, cooking, and his infectious smile. Thanks for leading me to God, Pops.

I dedicate the second third of this book to my Grandma, Shirley Lee. She loved all of her family members, especially us men. I miss our conversations about Bible stories and dreams, then watching you eat some cake. Because of you, I have good people skills.

I dedicate the last third of this book to Uncle David. A man after His own heart. He had a heart of gold, taking care of everyone else but himself. I miss his laugh, support, and random stories.

I dedicate this book to y'all because losing y'all forced me to write . . .

CONTENTS

PREFACE

An Impartation

God granted me His grace and mercy, allowing me to experience pivotal moments that have profoundly changed the trajectory of my life. I do not believe in coincidences, accidents, or luck because everything happens for a reason.

God created the heavens, the earth, and everything in this universe His way. Therefore, everything is all by design. I believe God intentionally handpicked your gender, race, circumstances, and biological family members without your consent for His divine plan for your life. Whether you believe in God or not is between you and God, but you are still a part of His divine plan. His plan for your life may be outside the scope of your understanding, but we must submit to Him to receive it. We must trust God and the process by believing we have a purpose in life and use our gifts to draw all men unto Him.

My problem was I did not know what my gifts were or what I was created to do until I started reading the Bible and writing. Also, I was angry with God because I did not understand why a lot of things were happening to me and my people, especially when we had a covenant with Him. I know that we as a people are far from perfect, but my life felt like I was damned if I did right and damned if I did wrong. I started reading the Bible in hopes of seeking the truth and some answers. I needed to know what His purpose for my life was and what I was created to do.

INTRODUCTION

Writing a book about my journey was never a plan of mine. This was a sheer sign of divine intervention within itself. I started writing this book in July of 2023, a year after losing my father, uncle, grandmother, and nearly my mother, all in 2022. My heart was still hurting from a divorce I experienced in 2021. Moreover, in 2020, the entire world was quarantined due to the coronavirus.

I was completely devastated and a shell of myself because the last three years of my life felt like I had spent them in solitary confinement. I am sure I appeared normal on the outside, but internally, I was grieving and struggling to keep myself together. I had a few legit things to complain about: my father was gone too soon, and he did not get to see me become a father. On top of that, I allowed my marriage to slip away, my loved ones were passing away, and time seemed to be flying by me.

Feeling depressed was an understatement. I turned to sex, weed, and therapy to help me cope with the trauma I experienced, but that only seemed to make matters worse. Although consented sex seemed to be a temporary stress reliever, it came with lust and soul ties that lasted longer than the temporary time of pleasure.

Once I sobered up from smoking, the trauma I suffered before smoking was still there; it hung around like a bad habit. And we all need someone to vent to, but my lack of connection with some of the therapists I sought out only sent me back into the quicksand.

I was at a crossroads in my life, and I needed some divine intervention. Reading and writing brought out the best in me. Reading the Bible and writing about the stories I read gave me a different perspective on life, and it was therapeutic.

My plan was to read the entire Bible, one chapter at a time, and write down what I got from it each time I read it. My motto became, "Read a chapter a day to keep the devil away," and it kept me motivated to do just that.

As I continued reading the Bible, I started noticing similarities and full circle moments, sort of like *déjà vu*. I realized that history was repeating itself, and there was no difference between what the people were going through back then in the Bible and what we are going through now as a people. In fact, we have somewhat of an advantage because the stories in the Bible are already written, and we can draw from them.

What I find more divine about me writing this book is that until recently, I was not an avid reader. My grammar was not the best, and the one time I wrote a story before this was in English class.

Math happened to be my favorite subject. Growing up, I viewed reading books as boring. Some books took too long to finish, and my attention span was short. I preferred watching a movie based on a novel versus reading about it. I am a visual learner, so I've gotta see it to believe it. Simply put, I viewed myself as an unlikely candidate to write a book.

As I continued to read and study the Living Word page by page, one chapter at a time, the stories began to come alive. I could visualize the stories coming together right before my eyes like a puzzle. God would choose an unlikely character to perform miracles during the darkest hours to show signs of His presence and divine intervention. The characters God chose to perform these miracles were human, flawed, and facing some sort of adversity, just like you and me.

For example, the children of Israel were taken captive as slaves in Egypt but were eventually freed by one of God's chosen characters. There were so many parallels between the children of Israel and *us*.

God chose mysterious characters and used unlikely objects to fulfill His plan throughout the Bible time after time. Their troubled times somehow prepared them for what was to come. So, if your faith is being tested due to troubling times, just know that if you are serving the God of Israel, He is preparing you for something bigger than what you can see. Know that He is preparing you to do something miraculous that will make a difference in your life and in the lives of others around you.

God gives the ones He has chosen divine intervention to protect them from darkness even when they see trouble heading in their direction. Once you realize the Hand of God intervening in your life, it becomes your full responsibility to execute His plan. It is your responsibility to play the cards God has dealt you, regardless of whether you like your hand or not. This will come with many obstacles in your life, but just know that God is not always there when you call Him, but He is always on time.

Also, obedience is better than sacrifice. And if you have not discovered your purpose yet or do not know why God created you, I recommend you seek to comprehend the Word of God, starting with Genesis.

Life is a journey full of ups and downs, and God provides balance. It takes time for things to develop and happen, but as long as you are alive and keep your trust and faith in God, He cannot fail you. Be patient with yourself, continue to strive for greatness, and trust the process. Turn your negatives into positives, and know that God is working things out for the greater good, no matter how difficult your journey may seem.

I struggled with understanding my purpose for most of my life. Meanwhile, I had close friends who knew exactly what they were born to do, and they wasted no time sharing their gifts with others. I thank God for allowing them to be my close friends because they kept me motivated and focused on pursuing my purpose. Through their gifts, I recognized that all things are possible.

Whether you are pursuing your purpose or attempting to figure it out, this book is for you. I wrote this book to shed light on my miraculous journey in hopes that it will inspire you to keep moving forward in pursuit of your purpose despite life's obstacles.

While reading the Bible, I became even more convinced that I had overcome all these trials and tribulations so I could share them with you. After all I went through and survived while growing up in South Central L.A., the fact that I can write about it is a blessing and miracle within itself.

At the point in my life when I finally found some surface and crawled out of the quicksand that had been pulling me under, there was no doubt in my mind that God had a bigger plan for me because I was still alive and in my right state of mind.

As history repeated itself, I saw God's hands in my life. I began to take note of His divine intervention and how His hands used me the same way His hands used the characters in the Bible. Just like those characters, I was grieving and frustrated with God over uncontrollable circumstances taking place, and I desperately needed a miracle. Then, God performed a blessing and a miracle by granting me the time and space to write.

Miraculously, during the time I started writing this book, I was in the middle of reading the Second Chronicles in the Bible, hence the title of this book, *South Central Chronicles Volume 1: Divine Intervention.*

CHAPTER ONE

THE CARDS THAT I WAS DEALT

July 2023, I was at home sitting in front of my laptop, waiting for my video therapy session. I was grieving over the passing of my father, grandma, uncles, and nearly my mother—which took place a few months ago in 2022.

My therapist never showed up for that session, and our schedules conflicted. I was grieving and looking for an outlet. I had run out of options and had no other choice but to call on the Lord. Suddenly, I grabbed a pen and started writing. I began writing about my journey and searching for my purpose.

As I started reflecting, I could not believe how fast time flies, it seems like it was just yesterday when me and Pops discussed death and now it was here . . .

ME & POPS:

I could remember it like it yesterday. One night me and my pops were driving home in his Chevy pickup truck, when a song by the Jackson 5 came on the radio. He turned up the volume, then looked at me and began singing, "I don't know how many stars there are up in the heavenly sky."

Immediately after the song went off, he said to me, "Son, everyone is going to die one day, including me and you, and no one knows when or how, but we will meet again up in the heavenly sky."

It was my introduction to death, and it was a very puzzling topic, to say the least. I was around seven or eight years old, and I had a hard time processing what dying or death meant. As I continued to ponder about it, my conclusion was that it did not apply to me or my family, so I had nothing to worry about, and life went on. Little did I know that time would fly by and no one was exempt from dying.

Fast forward to 2022, a few of my close loved ones who were near and dear to my heart had passed away, and all I had left were their memories. It felt like yesterday when me and my pops had our first conversation about death that night in the truck while bumping, "Maybe Tomorrow" by the Jackson 5, and now he had died, just as he predicted.

Losing someone close to me like my pops instinctively made me look at life differently and become more focus on executing my goals in life. I would often dream and drift on memories about my upbringing with him and all the lessons he taught me to prepare me for life with or without him. He had laid a solid foundation for his family to build on and the building started with me. He always reminded me that my last name was HALL, and he made sure that the "apple did not fall too far from the tree." My pops was a very well-rounded person and made sure we experienced love, pain, laughter, tears, music, food, extended family, road trips, amusement parks, shoes and clothes, money, celebrations, hard work, and God.

My pops was born in Buffalo, New York and raised in Watts, California, in a rigid town on the east side of South Central, Los Angeles. He was a carpenter and a perfectionist, especially when it came to his construction projects. His claim to fame was bragging about having a third-grade education but could build a house from the ground up.

He had many hobbies, like cooking, telling jokes, and singing. I miss him dearly; besides the inappropriate jokes, I miss hearing him playing his oldies music, and his no-bullshit attitude. He knew how to have a good time and made sure everyone around him was laughing and having fun, too.

When people ask me about my pops, I always tell them that even if he was not my pops, I would want to be friends with him and hope that God would allow us to cross paths in some type of way. There was never a dull moment with him, he was a very well-balanced individual. He kept God first, took care of his friends and family, handled his business, made money, and kept you laughing. He was very knowledgeable, and he made shit happen. He was in my everyday life since birth, and I always showed him that I was appreciative of him through my actions. I am his alter ego and vice versa.

He was a legend in his era and arguably one of the best to ever come out of Watts. He was handpicked by God to accomplish some amazing feats during his time on Earth. His tough love was enough, but his perspective on life, sense of humor, and personality were unmatched, I could not have scripted him any better. I could go on and on about him, but that is a story for another day. It was a privilege to have my pops in my life and I made sure not to take life for granted. I could see why my mom fell in love with him because he was the truth. The story is told that they met through their individual cousins over a good old card game of spades in South Central.

MOM AND ME:

My mom is a praying woman, a devoted wife and mother, and a helping hand to her extended family. She constantly puts everyone before herself. She could have easily been a counselor because she loves to talk, fuss, nag, and then pray for you.

Most of my childhood memories of me with her consists of us riding in the car, running errands, listening to her lecturing me about something I did wrong, during the entire car ride there and back. I was thankful for those lectures because they helped me put things in perspective, though they were very exhausting. I stayed in trouble, but she never gave up on me and kept lecturing and praying that one day I would wake up and get it right.

My mom's daily life was waking us up, getting us dressed for school, dropping us off at school, going to work, picking us up from school, helping one of our family members out, car lectures, taking us to our extra-curricular activities, running errands, preparing dinner, washing clothes, cleaning the house, getting us ready for bed, praying, quality time with Pops, and do it all over again the next day.

She was a machine; I never saw her break down, not once, and she did her best not to complain.

I could see why people wanted to take advantage of her because she was kind, and people sometimes take your kindness for weakness. Every once in a blue moon, you would see her break out of character and cuss someone out, and then start praying for them. She is a very thorough, witty, and selfless person.

My mother is a fraternal twin and had 12-15 siblings at one point in her life. She grew up in St. Louis, Missouri, and decided to move to South Central, Los Angeles, with her parents, siblings, and a few of her cousins.

Mom worked for the Department of Social Services for the L.A. County and retired early to take care of my Pops. She loved helping others out and would give her last without any questions. She grew up poor which motivated her to raise us up to have and want more out of life than she and her siblings had. Although, she did not have much growing up she made sure we always had enough. She would go out of her way so our childhood experiences were better than hers. At that time, all I had to offer was suspensions, notes, parent conferences, and phone calls from school. I did not think before acting up and I did not care about the consequences until it was too late. Life was all fun and games to me until my mom came to pick me up and I had to hear her nag the whole ride home, followed by a whooping or punishment by my Pops. Sometimes, I rather face my pop's belt than hear my mom nag. As soon as she picked me up from school, she would start off by saying, "I am tired of you getting in trouble at school. It is embarrassing to get phone calls from your school every day at my job. When are you going to wake up and realize everyone is not your friend, and they are trying to get you in trouble? You are smarter than that, so why can't you just ignore people?"

She was excellent at breaking everything down as if she was there.

And anytime I would offer a rebuttal, her response would be simple, "Just ignore people."

She put everything from a moral perspective and there was no winning with her. No matter how much I tried to bargain with her, she would not budge.

I still tried to explain, which made matters worse, then she would sigh and say, "You're just too damned determined to have it your way. You do not listen. You are too hard-headed," but she never gave up on me. She tried whooping me, but I would grab the belt and hold it until her energy drained.

If it was not for my mother's prayers, I do not know where I would be.

My prayer is that I give her some grandkids before the rapture, but if not, I am sure this book will suffice.

Overall, I was thankful to have both of my parents while growing up. As I got older, I realized that it is a blessing to have anyone in your life who loves you unconditionally and has your best interest at heart. No matter if they are biological family or not, count it as a privilege and never take anyone's love for granted because the streets don't love nobody.

SIBLINGS
THEM & ME

OLDEST SISTER

I have three biological sisters: two older and one younger. My oldest sister was cool when she wanted to be, but we always made sure to show love whenever she was around. We were a blended family and she opted to live with her biological mother instead of us. In my opinion, she should have chosen to live with us because she was Pop's first child, and we would all go out whenever she was with us. Also, she looks more like my Pops than any of us, but that's another argument between us for another day. She gave our Pops his first grandchild and assisted with taking care of him before he passed away.

OLDER SISTER

My second oldest sister was my very first friend in the world. We are 18 months apart, so by default, we grew up together. She is intellectually gifted and has always been ahead of her time. She was reading, writing, spelling, and counting at the age of three, before starting preschool. Once she started school, the principal wanted her to skip a grade or two, but my mother did not allow it for whatever reason.

I was very fortunate and blessed to be born right behind her. I soaked up almost everything that she did, which was mostly scholastics. She loved reading and would pick up on everything she saw and heard. When we were toddlers, my parents would try to surprise us by taking us somewhere fun and disguise it by spelling out where to one another, but my sister would pick up on it. Pops would say to my mom, let's go to the M-O-V- I-E-S and my sister would whisper to me, "We are going to the movies."

My sister introduced me to reading and we had every single Disney book with it's video cassette to match. She could read the book and follow the storyline, but I had to watch the movie to keep up. She taught me how to read, write, spell, and do arithmetic. We did everything together from playing video games, doing chores, doing homework, sharing rooms, and even getting into trouble.

This was the beginning of my bad behavior in school but my sister always had my back and never told on me. She stayed out of trouble, and whenever she did get in trouble, it had something to do with me.

She was an excellent leader, very loyal, and fearless. Most of the time she got picked on because she was so gifted and different from the rest of us. She would rather stay home and read a book instead of going outside to play, which frustrated me so I would pick on her by teasing her and calling her names which she did not stand for.

On top of being intelligent, she was down-to-earth, and could get physical with you, too. She gave me my first set of stitches on the right side of my head. For the rest of my life, I will wear a permanent bald spot on my head that was made by her. After that head injury, it seemed like my mom had separated us because we had different interests—she enjoyed indoor stuff while I was outside.

After middle school, she enrolled in an all-girls high school where she become freshman class president and salutatorian and graduated with honors. She received multiple academic scholarships to Division One universities across the country and graduated from the University of Notre Dame with honors. She was on the committee and was the chair of the dinner, which landed us on stage at Notre Dame with the president of the college. She was always recognized for her academic achievements at least twice a year throughout her career in school.

It was a privilege, an honor, and an unfair advantage to follow her lead. She introduced me to pop music, MacIntosh computers, and driving. Because of her, I became the freshman class president in high school at an all-boys school in Watts. The following semester I transferred to a co-ed public high school and tested in the math/science magnet program. I received an academic/athletic scholarship and graduated from the University of Saint Mary's with a bachelor's degree in business administration with an emphasis in marketing, just like her.

She had done her part, as the older sister, by leading me in the right direction and always having my back. If it was not for her, my comprehension and level of competition would not be where it is today. My ability to focus, love myself, and stand for what I believe in is all because of her. She showed me how to be a leader and how to know my worth. This was very important for me because I had someone watching and following my every move— my baby sister.

BABY SISTER

Five years after I was born, came my baby sister. I remember when the news was first told to me and my older sister. We both were excited; I wanted a baby brother, and she wanted a baby sister. Once we found out it was a girl, it was bittersweet for me. Bitter because I wanted a brother and sweet because a new baby was added to our family.

She was very adorable and immediately spoiled rotten. Whatever games my older sister and I were playing, and she wanted to play, we had to share it or give it to her. We would get in trouble if she cried or if anything happened to her. We had chores and she did not. I played the big brother role well by picking on her, teasing, agitating, and roughing her up every chance I got. I felt like it was my duty to make her tough on the outside but sweet on the inside. She was a little brat and always got her way, I did not like that one bit. I knew it was not her fault because she was the baby and being spoiled rotten just came with the territory. In her defense, she managed to stand up for herself and not allow me to bully her.

My older sister would play the referee and make sure that there was a mutual understanding. As we got older, we started to bond more as I continued to show her the ropes of life. I made sure she was exposed to the good, the bad, the ugly, and the beautiful—up close and personal.

I did my best to lead by example, but we were raised in two different eras and our gender differences made it difficult for us to relate to one another.

However, I knew she was watching me very closely. So, I had to get her up to speed with life as I knew it.

My Pops would always brag about my baby sister being the most gifted out of all of his children. She could sing, write songs, design clothes, and create almost anything from scratch. When I realized how gifted she was, I did my best to keep her inspired by always achieving something, hoping she would follow suit.

Every time I got a fresh idea, I would share it with her, and she would help me flesh it out. We started a clothing line together and we are always brainstorming new business ideas.

She has grown up to be a very creative, God-fearing, devoted wife and mother. I am so proud of her because she is a good friend, a prayer warrior, a spiritual advisor, a songwriter, a singer, and manages to do things her way without compromising. She gave our parents their first grandchild which is a blessing. We still argue from time to time because I must make sure she understands that I am her big brother and she must follow my lead by God's design.

EXTENDED FAMILY MEMBERS

My father's side is made up of scholars, intense, firm, and militant-like people. My father was the last born in his immediate family, he had three older sisters and one older brother. He practically grew up with his nieces and nephews because they were all born and raised around the same time, which forged their close bonds. At the time I was born, my grandma—his mom—had passed away, so I never got a chance to meet her, but my grandpa's presence made up for her absence. My grandpa was an eccentric man full of energy. He had many talents, and he did not take any prisoners.

He served in the U.S. Army and after he served, he ran multiple businesses, across South Central L.A. I witnessed his discipline style—blunt, argumentative, and sometimes physical—he was all about tough love.

Every time we went to my grandpa's house in Watts, it was always love. The community was full of love, respect, raw talent, and competition. Everyone seemed to be gifted, especially in music, sports, and hustling. It was a "no-holds-barred" type of environment, and everyone knew one another like family.

The entire neighborhood knew about the "Hall Family," and when they found out who my father, grandpa, and family was, they received me with open arms. It was always love and respect amongst each other and whenever there was an issue, it got squashed by throwing them hands. You had to know how to fight because you were going to get tested at any given time for whatever reason. The community is self-governing, and the people are very genuine.

My older cousins made sure we knew how to protect ourselves, stand up for each other, and keep money in our pockets. On the weekends, one of my older cousins would round up some of the kids on the block and take us out to his house in Riverside, a suburb outside of the hood, to expose us to a more modern lifestyle. It was like going on a field trip with a select few who were down for whatever. I learned a lot about myself, life, and my cousins during those weekend trips in Riverside. As we grew older, we always made time to hang out and pick up where we left off. And we would fall off where we went wrong, or life would force us to love from a distance.

My mother's side was much like father's side, times 100. My grandma and grandpa ushered in about 15 kids, about 30 grandkids, and approximately 60 great-grandchildren.

In South Central, whenever we gathered for a birthday celebration there were about 40 plus people, roughly 30 kids and 10 adults. At any given time, we were forced to go outside and play because we were too overwhelming for the adults. Not to mention, the main meet up house was a one-bedroom shack sandwiched in between a car lot and a bar off Florence Avenue, on arguably one of the busiest public streets in the world. My aunty house was one of my favorite places to visit growing up because there was never a dull moment. Imagine 20-30 kids mobbing together, up and down the street, looking for something to get into. We were exposed to it all and there was always something going on whether it was in traffic, on the back streets, in the house, or at the park. We were like sponges, soaking up everything we saw, and it programmed us on how to survive anywhere in the world.

Every time we all linked up it was a celebration. My mom and her siblings are so close to each other that they had given birth to most of their kids in August. I tease my cousins about being conceived during the holidays in November and December.

My grandpa on my mom side is one of my favorite people of all time. He is down to earth, smooth, and a family man. He is everyone's father and grandpa. We keep up with each other on a weekly basis, mainly through sports, video games, and stories. I admired his ability to keep up with the changes of time, while maintaining a simple lifestyle. He is living proof that longevity is possible and I am determined to make it to his age one day.

Spending equal time with both sides of the family was very rewarding and testing. They are my "Royal Flush."

AND THEN THERE WAS ME

Whenever I wasn't writing, I would go to the beach to reflect and clear my mind.

One day I was standing at the shoreline, soaking up the scenery, with my feet in the water. As I gazed at this beautiful body of work that God created, I realized that we were fortunate enough to be literally living at the edge of the Earth, right before it curved.

The ocean reminded me of my life, on a constant cycle, with unpredictable waves. Sometimes, the waves would come in rough, and knock me down, but I got right back up. Other times, the waves would come in gently, and dissipate at the shoreline. And whenever I looked down (for too long), the illusionary motion in the ocean made it hard to decipher. If I was moving forward or standing still, until God lifted up my head to pull me out of it. His love is so magnetic that it slowly had pulled me into the ocean, as I fought to keep my head above water, but I was still moving forward. The magnetic force that had pulled me into the ocean was as real as the hands that had pulled me out of my mother's womb.

MY CAKE DAY

On January 29th, I was pulled out of the womb, weighing seven pounds, six ounces, at twenty-one inches in length. From the moment I came out of the womb, I felt both love and pressure. Pressure from the birth itself, and love from the nurses who took turns holding me while my mother recovered. I was a cry-baby, and no one could hold me to calm me. I kept that same energy when we arrived home from the hospital, only a select few members held me: my parents, grandparents, two aunts, one from each side of my family, anyone outside of them, and I was crying and pleading to get out of their grips.

At least that is what was told to me, and I believed it because I have always had no problem expressing myself. No matter if it was good or bad energy that was coming from me or other people, I felt the energy. Whether the pressure was from me or other people, I could feel both good and bad present. I could not control how others responded to it, but I was always in control of my response to any energy in my presence. No matter if it was good or bad, I felt the energy.

THE LEARNING CENTER

Between the ages of two and five, I attended the learning center on 41st Place and Central, located on the east side of South Central. Later I found out it was around the corner from the Dunbar Hotel, a famous Black jazz spot from back in the days.

At the learning center, I had trouble sleeping during nap time, which kept the other kids up. I would laugh and play, ignore the teachers, and run around until my assigned teacher would come pick me up, lay me down, rub my back, and sing to me until I fell asleep. It was the same routine day in and day out but this one particular day was different. And this one day is the last fond memory I would have with my assigned teacher. I was running around avoiding nap time as usual, she finally caught me, and made me lay down with the rest of the kids. She began her regular routine rubbing my back and singing to me, to calm me down, while the other kids were already in a slumber.

Then, she silently asked me, "When is your birthday?"

I said, "January 29th."

Then she giggled and said, "You are a natural born leader, like Dr. King, because y'all are born in the same month."

The problem was I had no idea who Dr. King was, I just wanted to play and have fun with the other kids.

As time went on, I slowly but surely started hearing about. Dr. King and his cause for standing up for our civil rights, boycotting, and preaching. The brother was a wordsmith and sounded like he was speaking in another language. He was honored with a national holiday, a monument, and globally recognized for receiving a Nobel Peace Prize but was still assassinated. He died for a cause and will forever be etched in history for, his "I Have A Dream" speech at the Million Man March, but that did not matter to me. He had lived out his purpose and I was on a quest to figure out mine.

WADSWORTH ELEMENTARY SCHOOL

Life in South Central L.A. was all fun and games, especially in grade school, where I got into the most trouble. Once my parents dropped me and my older sister off at the learning center, we were inseparable, until it was time for us to go to the big school next door at Wadsworth Elementary School. When we walked over to Wadsworth, my older sister joined the third graders while I stayed with the first graders.

Separating us really hurt my feelings. I would intentionally finish my work early, ask to use the restroom, and roam the hallways looking in each classroom until I found her. I would get her attention, which disturbed the class, and sprint back to my classroom before her teacher caught me.

The times that I was not allowed a hall pass, I would crack jokes and distract others from learning until I was sent to the principal's office.

Me and a group of friends would chase girls around, crack jokes on each other, and ditch school to go to the candy house off campus. I was getting in trouble and suspended weekly. My loved ones were concerned about my behavior issues because they knew trouble in South Central was always lurking, and I was not hard to find. My parents and family members attempted to warn me that life for a Black man was not all fun and games and that I better get my act together before it was too late. I was oblivious to the troubles lurking in the streets of South Central L.A., until that one time I saw it for myself.

THE 92 RIOTS

I remember it like it was YESTERDAY. I was standing on my Grandpa's front porch with my cousins in Watts, watching South Central go up in flames, and hearing the helicopters chopping through the air. At the time, I had no clue what was going on, until it was time to ride through the mayhem. You could feel the tension in the streets from angry protesters and non-Black store owners. It was literally hell on Earth, sparked by a racist store owner who took a young Black girl's life over a bottle of orange juice and ignited by a Black man named Rodney King, who was beaten by racist cops on national TV and later acquitted. What is the irony of two Black men with the same last name "King" being the focal point of racial tension that resulted in riots?

Every day we had to drive through the heavy racial tension that plagued the streets of South Central, even after the smoke had cleared. The streets were filled with racist crooked cops, angry protestors, and crooks. We were hoping and praying that we did not get caught up in a melee or pulled over by the cops.

This was my first taste of systemic racism and a reality check that shaped my outlook on life as a Black kid growing up in the ghetto of South Central L.A.

Little did I know, this was only the beginning of the problems lurking around, as an even deadlier agenda was on the horizon that would have us targeting each other through street politics.

Even though this wicked agenda was targeting us minorities, it would not slow me down from misbehaving, having fun, and enjoying my youth.

Eventually, Wadsworth Elementary and my parents had enough of my misbehavior until I was kicked out of the public school district. To me, I was acting out of instinct and being a rambunctious boy like the rest of the kids—but my elders and teachers saw it different.

Maybe I was hardheaded, due to the two major head injuries that resulted in getting stitches and staples plunged into my scalp before the age of eight. So, they had to charge it to my head and not my heart.

SAINT ANSELM

After getting kicked out of the Los Angeles Unified School District, my parents checked me into a Catholic school, and for the first time I was permanently separated from my older sister. It was located on the west side of South Central off Florence and Van Ness.

My mother would drop me off early in the morning at one of my favorite aunties' home off Florence, then I would catch the bus back and forth to school by myself. I was eight years old, catching the public bus alone. I enjoyed it because I learned the names of the streets throughout South Central, and the random people who got on and off the bus were funny, to say the least.

My new school provided me with discipline, structure, and compassion which was something I was missing. I started going there in the third grade which was one of the pivotal moments that changed the trajectory of my life. It was a fresh start for me and a new way of life. Unlike the public school, we wore uniforms and went to mass every week. The school was much smaller than the public school I previously attended, and the way they ran their program was different, too.

We were rewarded for our good grades, which kept me motivated and focused. The girls seemed classier, and everyone wore name brand shoes to make up for having to wear uniforms. There were school dances, academic contests, organized sports, everyone knew each other, and I seemed to fit right in from day one.

I was clicking on all cylinders and was starting to get the hang of life, as time moved on. My daily routine was going to school and participating in extracurricular activities Monday through Friday, which kept me focused. I would alternate spending Friday nights at one of my cousin's or friend's house, but I had to be back home by Saturday night for church on Sunday mornings. Church was mandatory on Sundays, followed by some sort of family activities such as the movies or a restaurant.

Life was fun and I felt like it was getting better until tragedy struck close to home, as a new deadly agenda was plaguing the streets of L.A. and the surrounding cities.

SOUTH CENTRAL L.A. CULTURE
not like us . . . .

On the way home from church, the corner of my street was yellow taped off. Me and Pops walked to the corner to see what had happened, and my mentor was on the scene. He told me that a young Black teenager who lived on our street, was shot and killed at the corner, while walking to the liquor store with his family. I asked him why he was killed, he said he didn't know but that police said it was "street gangs."

Suddenly, my attention shifted from fun and games to a new reality—gang members. Some gang members represented in red while their rivals represented in blue which was no different from the Democrats and the Republicans that we see on TV today.

At the time, I did not realize that this was a setup from the start aimed to keep us divided and conquered through street politics." It was a life for a life, and in the end, no one would benefit from it because someone would end up dead while the other one would end up doing life in jail. Some young members already thought going to jail was a rite of passage and an allegiance to their gang ties versus realizing the original purpose of joining a gang was for unity and to protecting people within their communities. Joining a gang became the normal trap for a lot of misunderstood individuals in South Central L.A.

To make matters worse, if you decided not to join, you were still targeted by your address or affiliations. To add insult to injury, we were already living in close proximity to one another which made it easy to pull off drive-by's and target one another. Anything could tick someone off in the streets and the whole summer could get ugly.

The weather was always sunny, so young people were always outside in the streets having fun. Either at a backyard function, or somewhere around the way watching random "clown-dancers" pull up, hop out, and start battling in the middle of the street. I am pretty sure that there are many unique street cultures across the globe, but not like us.

In South Central L.A., the beach was right down the street, so we partied there, or went there to wash away our sins. In these same streets, it was a deadly battle going on that left many loved ones traumatized for life. But who could you blame? The government or the people in the streets for carrying out this vicious agenda?

At least blaming it on the government felt like the right thing to do when the sad truth is blaming things on other people does not get you very far. At some point, you must be accountable for your own actions, show love, and be the change you want to see. This is easier said than done because we all know the streets don't love nobody. But this type of cowardly mentality to kill each other was doing more harm than anything else. Being a gang member was a huge distraction from our God-given purpose.

The streets were worse than signing up for the military, so a lot of young people joined the military to escape poverty, while others tapped into their God-given gifts to escape this reality. It was a constant struggle for anyone not to get caught up in the street life while attempting to figure out their God-given gifts.

Life was rough because resources were limited, but it forced us to work with what we had, hoping it would someday payoff, before the streets consumed you.

Personally, I could have cared less about systemic racism, the crabs in the buckets, and street politics because I feared God.

I started believing that God sent us here to break some molds, right some wrongs, and transition into the next realm. Having a spiritual relationship with God was the only thing that made sense to me. The way I saw it, there was no way that anyone could figure out this intricate world on their own, we all need some Divine Intervention. As complicated as all of this sounds, it was still all good in the hood.

We were literally living life on the edge of the Earth, off the Pacific Coast Ocean, right before it curved. There was never a dull moment growing up in the trenches with my family and friends.

Every time we linked up it was a party. With family, we would sit around and share funny stories, go to house parties, and ride bikes across town. Although the streets were dangerous, they were our playgrounds. We played dominoes, shot dice, and flossed our latest Jordans.

It was all good in the hood, we were young, wild, and living carefree.

The homies on my street always had money, women, low riders, and oldies. My neighbor was the local DJ, so we were always hustling at a party, every weekend. Most of my childhood homies became members but I remained the same. I did my best to be cautious while hanging around them because I knew that I was guilty by association. So, I remained aware and out of the way.

Whenever I would get too comfortable hanging out, a few of my Mexican compadres reminded me to be careful and to stay on the right track.

Instead, I embraced the other side of South Central L.A. culture. It was arguably the best place to grow up in but like Pac said, "You gotta be there to know it when everybody wanna see." It was summer camp at St. Andrews Park, the pool at Green Meadows or Jessies Owens, followed by Burger Palace.

At night, after celebrating the Lakers winning another championship, we would party at "The Current Affair" in Inglewood, World on Wheels, or "The Soda Pop," in the Crenshaw District. After hours, we would cruise down Crenshaw, and watch lowriders and motorcycle clubs flaunt their stuff. South Central L.A. was life in the fast lane with no intentions of slowing down.

During these times, I had made up my mind to hold my own, figure out my God-given purpose, and thrive in this fast-paced lifestyle. I thought I had it all figured out in middle school until I saw it up close and personal.

MIDDLE SCHOOL: UP CLOSE & PERSONAL

I had established a solid reputation amongst my peers in the streets for having a good time and holding my own.

Life was progressing slowly but surely; I was in middle school and thriving in the right direction when a new kid on the block popped up. He lived around the corner and was new to the east side, we ended up competing against each other in sports, and eventually became friends.

We had a lot in common, we both played basketball, and was going to the same school on the west side of town.

Although, I had been going to St. Anselm for a while, he fit right in as if he had been already attending school there. He was a grade ahead of me, and I was thankful to have someone from the east side to associate with. It was a dope experience to have someone you know who lived on the same side of town as you and have a few things in common with you. For a year straight I watched him dominate in organized basketball and in streetball. I would bet on him against my friends in the local neighborhood and win every time. He had handles, with an unorthodox shot that started off well behind his head, like Jake Shuttlesworth from the movie "He Got Game" which made it difficult for any defender to block, and his shot would somehow go in eight out of ten times. You could not beat him, so you were better off joining him. He was my secret weapon and for a year straight, and he went everywhere I went and vice-versa. I would try to take him everywhere I go.

A year had flown by, I was in the seventh grade, he was in the eighth grade, and we were operating like brothers. He was about to graduate and transition into high school.

I remember this particular day like it happened yesterday, my parents were mumbling in the front seat when they picked me up from my cousin's house that evening, before they broke the news. Son, your friend was gunned down in the streets, and died on Vermont, in front of the Smart & Final® store.

I could not believe it. I had just saw him in good health, laughing, and playing with his blue nosed pit bull puppy. He told me that he was going to Six Flags Magic Mountain, so how did he die? And where is he now?

I had no idea how to process the death of someone so close and near and dear to my heart. I was immediately stunned and shocked, but I had to see it to believe it. My parents went back and forth about allowing me to see his lifeless body laying stiff in a casket.

I stood motionless, traumatized by the sight of my friend body laying stiff in the casket. His casket was eye level for me, an up, close, and personal experience my mind will never forget.

I stared at his chest, mouth, and nostrils, waiting for him to breath or move. His eyes were mostly closed, but I could see a slither of his white eyeballs. His face was blank, his mouth was shut, and he looked as if he was resting.

I stared at his body for a long time, wondering what he was thinking, or if he could think, and what was going to happened to him next. For a long time after that, I imagined him appearing in my house at night, standing there staring at me, like I did to him while he was laying lifeless in the casket.

To this day I think about his mother, wondering how she is currently doing and hoping that she is still living.

8TH GRADE

It was the start of eighth grade, and a lot had changed in a short span of time. My hormones were raging as I started to explore the different body parts of a girl. I was kissing, hugging, and rubbing on the girls like it was nobody's business, especially at the parties.

My parents signed me up for Pop Warner football, to keep me focused, which was my first time ever playing in pads. It was sometimes intimidating but my heart would not let me stop. I was very competitive and was not afraid of contact. I instinctively avoided collisions, as the coaches relied on me to return kicks and cover wide receivers.

My Pop Warner coach was a firefighter and a mentor to us all. He gave this speech one day after practice and it would stick with me for the rest of my life. We were all taking a knee and he stood before us, "Not everyone of you will make it to the pros. In fact, only one out of 100 players that you see out here will make it as a professional athlete. The rest of you will become a decent human being, with respect, and a productive man for your community. I am here to teach you how to be discipline and not quit on yourselves nor each other. You may not understand it now but someday you will."

At the time I did not fully understand the message he was conveying, but I could read between the lines.

As far as school, I was still progressing and doing well. The major topic of discussion amongst my peers was high school. The last semester as an eighth grader was a blur. One of my best friends moved to Atlanta, but I still had a handful of friends within my reach.

During my last year at St. Anselm, my parents emphasized the importance of keeping my name clean by staying out of trouble and keeping good grades. They told me from here on out my reputation would follow me wherever I went, and it would determine if I was going to get a good job and a full scholarship into college. So, I made sure to pass all my classes with A's and to avoid the law in the streets by minding my business. I was extra careful when it came to staying away from trouble, at least I thought I was, but trouble was always lurking.

That summer, right after graduating from middle school, was crucial for me as it would reshape my thought process for the rest of my life.

BLURRED LINES

It was an average sunny day on the block, a group of us were riding our bikes around the neighborhood. We ended up riding to a vacant house around the corner and broke inside.

One of my friends pulled out some weed and started rolling up it. I was very apprehensive but wanted to try it out. I did not know how to smoke, but my friend was eager to show me. He demonstrated and passed it to me.

Afterward, we left out of the house, jumped on our bikes, and headed to the store. My friends rushed into the store and grabbed all of the snacks, while I stood there and watched. They asked me if I wanted something but suddenly, I became incoherent. Once we got outside of the store and back on our bikes, my chain had popped off, and for the first time I could not figure out how to fix it. My friends laughed at me, while figuring out that I was high.

Suddenly, I heard this buzzing in my ear, that sounded like screeching metal. My vision became blurry, as I could not control this weird experience. I made it to my friend's yard where they proceeded to laugh and crack jokes at me, when nothing was even funny. I felt like Smokey on "Friday," when the Mexican homies were laughing at him while he was tripping in the streets. They were annoying me, so I saw some other friends down the street in their yard, playing catch with the football. I rushed down the street and asked if I was acting weird or different.

One of the guys responded, no, then started laughing at me, too, as the chain had popped off my bike again, and I was still trying to pedal. Suddenly, I became paranoid and darted across the street to my house right before almost getting hit by a taxi driver. He slammed on the brakes and honked the horn.

When I got in the house, my mom and siblings were gone, and my pops was in his room. I told him that I had a headache and was going to sleep. I laid in my bed but could not sleep. My mind was racing in circles, as I wondered when the high would subside. The constant noise outside and around me became amplified from the airplanes overhead, to Mariachi music, dogs barking, and my Pop's TV show. My heart was throbbing fast, and I could hear and feel every heartbeat. After hours of lying there, I could not distinguish if the noise in the background was in my head or actually happening in real time, those lines were blurred. All I could do is pray and ask God to sober me up.

It felt like my high lasted for days and the lack of control over my thoughts and actions had kept me sober.

That same summer before high school, more trouble would find me. My parents were trying to figure out what type of school to send me to. I campaigned to go to a public high school, but they were undecided until this day near the end of summer.

STREET FIGHTS & JAIL TIME

There was a skateboard crew that was predominantly made up of Hispanic kids throughout the neighborhood. They skated throughout the hood no less than five members deep at a time. They would congregate at the corner and grind on the edge of the curb and do tricks in the middle of the street. We were a bike crew of three to four Black kids at a time.

Every time we ran into the skateboard crew we would clash and pick fights with each other, just for the hell of it. This one time, I was on the main stage as I squared up against one of the main members of the skateboard crew. He decided to use his skateboard as a weapon, took a calculated swing but missed me, and dropped his skateboard right in front of me. I quickly picked up his skateboard and swung it right across

25

his face, knocking him out cold. As I was running off, I could hear the police sirens and a firm voice over a loud speaker. The police handcuffed me, and took me to the police station and booked me for assault. This was my first time being detained, and all I could think about was Pops, while hearing my mom's nagging voice in my head.

I sat there for hours wondering what was going to happen to me, how I had become a statistic, and if I was ever going to make it to high school.

I tried to think up any excuse to get the attention of one of the deputies, but they were not buying it. I asked if I could at least call home, so my parents would not be worried about me, and they allowed me to call. Somehow, my parents were able to get me out of there and the charges were later dropped, and I was a free man.

Once I got home, I put myself on punishment and vowed never to get arrested again. I was ready for high school and a brand-new start. That arrest marked a turning point in my life, as I no longer viewed myself as an innocent child but more of an immature teenager.

Later that summer I found out that I was going to attend Verbum Dei High School, an all-boys Catholic school in Watts. It was a school that my Godmom sent her son to, where he excelled in football and got a full scholarship to the University of Nebraska. Verb were known for challenging academics and sports. Their football program was serious with weight-training, conditioning drills, and their arduous "two-a-days."

As my first semester of high school arrived, and I thought I knew it all. I had experienced riots, racial tension, being kicked out of school, street gangs, burying my peers, partying, having a girlfriend, catching the bus by myself, playing tackle football, blurred lines, and going to jail. I was thirteen, but little did I know I did not know nothing at all.

CHAPTER TWO

HIGH SCHOOL: VERB & THE PREP

During my freshman year at Verbum Dei, I got all A's, and became my freshman's class president. My older sister was my inspiration. She, too, was her freshman's class president, salutatorian, and received multiple scholarships to prestigious universities across the country.

All I wanted to do was keep up. I was a scholar in the classroom but was not much of a factor on the football field. I made the roster, but my inexperience kept me on the sidelines. It was my second year of playing tackle football, and at the high school level it was more mental than physical. I took mental reps on the sidelines and convinced myself that I would be ready by next season.

Off the football field, I was a stud. As the freshman class president, I was responsible for assisting with coordinating social activities, such as school parties. One of the most memorable experiences at Verb were the parties. All the student bodies at the local Catholic high schools in Compton, L.A., Inglewood, and Westchester would party inside the host gym chaperoned by the parents. Verb was the last place to host a dance because the local bloods from the Nickerson Gardens would come and crash the party.

I had so much fun at Verb, but their football program was cancelled the following year for whatever reason, and I convinced my parents to enroll me at the prep, a co-ed public school at the edge of South Central L.A.

THE PREP- WASHINGTON PREP

It was my second semester of my freshman year, and I had a few cousins from both sides of my family who were already attending the prep.

Initially, I was shell-shocked because it had been a longtime since I have seen so many students on campus all at once. There were so many students enrolled at the prep, that they had to split us up into three tracks (A-Track, B-Track, and C-Track), based off our address. I ended up being on A-track which was known for its traditional school schedule, with winter and summer breaks off. There were only two tracks allowed at a time, and each track spent an equal amount of time together throughout the year. We attended six classes a day, one hour per class, Monday through Friday.

That summer after my freshman year, I joined the junior varsity football team at the prep and was eager to assist with changing the narrative of the prep football program from losing to winning. The transition from Verb to the Prep was simple, because one of my friends transferred with me, and I became close friends with three of my teammates through competing.

I was maturing and feeling the best I had ever felt. I was starting on both sides of the football, my grades were good, and I had met this pretty girl at my first high school party. She attended a different high school, but we talked and hung out whenever we could.

THE BIRDS AND THE BEES

I remember the conversation with my Pops like it was yesterday. We were outside cleaning out the back of his work truck and he suddenly asked me about my girlfriend. He wanted to know if I had "reached home base with a helmet on," if you know what I mean.

I reluctantly responded with a lie by saying that all we do is talk on the phone and kiss whenever we hung out.

He could see right through me and knew I was lying. He was not angry but very firm and said, "Son, please use protection if you are going to be doing things that you are not supposed to be doing. You do not want to end up like me, on child support. The government will take almost all of your paycheck, before it touches your hand for 18 years, and you will be fucked. It is not worth it son. Do not have a baby out of wedlock. I'm trying to tell you what God loves."

His last words of not having a baby out of wedlock and being on child support would stick with me for the rest of my life. I did not want to disappoint my Pops. I did my best to focus on school and football, but my hormones were raging out of control.

DON'T FUMBLE THE ROCK

I was starting to make a name for myself on and off the football field. On the football field, I was fearless and could hold my own the same way I did off the field. However, one of the biggest plays that I'd ever made in a game on the field would have me questioning myself for the rest of my life.

We were on defense, and I was playing corner back on our side of the field, in front of the cheerleaders. The ball was thrown in my direction, I jumped up and intercepted it, and as soon as my feet touched the ground—the ball mysteriously popped out of my hands. There was nothing in front of me but green grass and a touchdown. The other team picked up the fumble and scored. Another lost for the prep.

When the game was over, I headed to the sideline and asked one of my teammates what happened, he said, "You fumbled the rock," and the coach mumbled, "I hope he doesn't fumble his potential," with a smirk on his face.

But how? I had it in my possession.

Over the next 20 years of my life, every time I messed up a good opportunity, this mysterious fumble would come back to haunt me. It was one of those defining moments that had me questioning my capabilities, on and off the field. Am I a playmaker or a must-play? Regardless, I was eager to make a name for myself, on and off the field.

During that summer, I went to summer school, trained hard to play varsity football, and hung out with my girlfriend.

At this point in my life, we were sexually active and exchanging more than soul-ties. She was pregnant and my heart sunk to my stomach when I received the news.

There was no way we could bring this baby into this world and my Pops would kill me if he even found out, we had just talked about the birds and the bees.

"We gotta get an abortion."

She was in her first trimester when I found out, and the doctor said that we had barely made the cut off time for the abortion. I remember sitting in the waiting room as she walked out of the procedure room with her head down and in tears. We eventually stopped dating and became friends, but it did not end well, she wished me bad luck, but I did not believe in luck.

I was a murderer and didn't even realize it, until now.

1ST SEMESTER OF 11TH GRADE

It was football season again and I had made it onto the varsity team. It was a team blended with size, speed, talent, and heart—but we lacked the winning spirit. Washington Prep's varsity football team was known around the city of Los Angeles for having a losing record year after year, and every school scheduled us for their homecoming game.

I was undersized with one of the biggest hearts on the team but was a bench warmer, as I pleaded with the coach, up and down the sideline of every game to put me in, but he just laughed and sarcastically stated I was too little, and would get injured.

I had heard this story a few times before, I was easily underestimated but, I wanted it that way, I was definitely a sleeper. The coaches "no" did not stop me from me from stalking him on the sidelines in every game. Then, one game during the fourth quarter I told the coach that we were not going to win, so he might as well put me in. The score would be 45-0 at halftime, we were losing almost every game by halftime, so I had nothing to lose. Quiet as kept, I was thankful not to get put in the games because I didn't want to be put on someone's highlight reel.

Then one homecoming game, he had a change of heart and decided to put me in. It was a tied game in the fourth quarter, with seconds left on the clock, and we were defending on the goal line. They thought we would be an easy win, but we put our nuts on the line this game.

So, there I was on the goal line rushing in on a corner back blitz and I collided with the running back right before he crossed the goal line, "mano y mano," until one of my teammates came flying in and injured me, just as the coach had predicted. I was helped off the field and then taken to a local hospital. It was literally a freak accident, but the doctors assured me that I would recover and had nothing to worry about.

I immediately thought about the bad luck my ex-girlfriend had wished earlier that year, after the abortion. I was thankful to be alive but in the following years, my faith was definitely tested.

2ND SEMESTER OF 11TH GRADE

It was the second semester of my junior year and I wanted to run track to get faster for football. Outside of street races, this was the first time I had ever raced in an organized setting. Track and field is a team sport, it takes the entire team to win, just like in football. I was fast and had endurance, but track and field is more about the heart. Literally, my heart would be pumping out of my chest every time I ran, but I was in love with competing. I loved the challenge of pushing myself past the finish line even when I was dizzy, out of breath, and near to fainting. I ran the 100, 200, 400, 4x1, and the 4x4. Somehow, I qualified for the city prelims in the 400 meters event alone. I was shocked because I was not keeping up with my stats. I did not get past the city prelims, but it reminded me that I was definitely a playmaker, on and off the field.

I was clearly underestimating my talents and too nonchalant to care. My focus was on partying, fashion, and girls during that entire summer before my senior year.

1ST SEMESTER OF 12TH GRADE

The first three years of high school flew bye, and I could not believe that I was a senior and was on my way to adulthood.

It was the beginning of football season and my time to shine. I was finally a starter on the varsity team and played on both sides of the ball, including the kick returner.

I was one of the fastest on the team and had a magnet for the ball. I loved hearing my name announced on the loudspeaker, so I made sure I was in on every play. I scored in almost every game we played and made key tackles on defense but never kept a record of my stats. I just wanted to play football, win games, and be an impact player.

There was one game where I stood out, but I did not realize it until the Mexican homies next door called me into their house. It was a Saturday morning and we had just lost a close game the night before to Long Beach Cabrillo. He opened the Los Angeles Times newspaper to the high school sports section and pointed out my name under the All-purpose section for scoring a 92-yard kickoff return, interception, numerous tackles, and a force fumble.

I could not believe it. I had to read it a couple times before I ran home and shared the news with my family and friends. The four of my homies were proud of me as we celebrated that whole day by hanging out and later going to the club.

It was a proud moment for me that was unplanned. I started wondering if there was any other news written about me from previous games because no one was checking. I knew that I was good but not good enough for recognition because all we did was lose, and the student body did not care until this one morning.

It was a regular school morning, and the entire student body was in their homerooms as the speaker buzzed to get everyone's attention for the usual announcements. The announcer went through the list and suddenly recognized me. I had made it on second team All-Marine League for both offense and defense in football. I was just as shocked as everyone else when I heard my name and could not believe it. I must have really balled out and wondered what my overall stats were that nobody was keeping up with.

Over the next few weeks, recruiters from Portland State University, Humboldt State, and Montana State came to my school to visit me and called me out of class to discuss my plans for college. They wanted a package deal that included me and one of my other teammates but for whatever reason things did not go as planned and the offers were rescinded.

2ND SEMESTER OF 12TH GRADE

Instead of participating in track and field, during my senior year, I decided to get a job at Ralph's grocery store to help me pay for my senior expenses. I got my driver's license, and my older sister left me her car while she went off to college. I was privileged to have a car during the last semester of my senior year, but it came with expenses such as gas, car insurance, and preventative maintenance. However, I did not care because I was driving and becoming a responsible young man. I worked that job from the beginning of the year up until it was time to graduate.

Nonetheless, I graduated from high school, walked the stage, and received my diploma. I was on my way to college and making history for myself and my family. High school was finally over, and I felt ready for adulthood. Three of my friends decided to join the service, while my other friend and I decided to go to college.

LIFE IN THE FAST LANE

The summer after graduating from high school, my Pops took me to the car lot and bought my first car —a Z28 Chevy Camaro. I was never into cars so; I had no idea what the Camaro was known for. We learned the transmission was slipping so, we immediately took it to the shop.

Once I got it out of the shop, I decided to take it for a test drive to see what the hype was all about. I got to the stop sign at the corner of my block, put the left blinker on and smashed the gas pedal to beat the oncoming traffic that was coming in opposite directions. I instantly lost control of the steering wheel as the Camaro fish tailed, and I quickly jammed the brakes before hitting the car that was parked next to me on the street.

I had panicked and underestimated the speed and power the Chevy Camaro possessed. Simultaneously, I screamed out of joy as the screeching tires and V8 engine ignited my adrenaline rush. Little did I know that the Z28 Chevy Camaro was a chick magnet. I received attention everywhere I went, especially after hours on Crenshaw. I made sure to keep my priorities in place by putting school first and not the chicks.

CHAPTER THREE

COLLEGE

It was the Fall of 2003 when I checked into Pasadena City College (PCC) to play football, and it was an hour commute from my home in South Central L.A. to Pasadena, California. That hour's drive alone gave me time to reflect on my future and a piece of mind away from the streets of South Central L.A. For the first two years at PCC, I focused on getting my general electives out of the way, so that I could focus on my major classes once I transferred to a four-year university. My main focus was getting a full-time scholarship and becoming one of the first males in my family to graduate from college.

On the field, I thought I was the man until I realized there were other recruits from all over the country who were bigger, stronger, faster, and more experienced than me.

The collegiate level was more about the mental aspect of the game versus raw talent. Although I had the heart and speed to compete, I was missing the mental component which dealt with situational football, alignment, making the right decisions at the right time, and executing the plays.

The coaches wanted me to redshirt or sit out my freshman year, but I was too determined to play and finish school. I was recruited to play running back but there were already a few running backs ahead of me, one who eventually became a professional NFL running back for the

Cleveland Browns, and broke Jim Brown's single game rushing record. There was no way I was going to get any playing time as a running back so, I was quickly transformed into a cornerback.

Before every practice, the team would line up in rows to stretch, while the head coach walked through and gave his familiar speech. He had a very simple philosophy, and to this day, I apply it in my everyday life, especially when writing this book. He said, "Get better by 1% every day until you reach 100%. I instantly understood that if you have a goal, do at least one thing every day towards reaching that goal, until you have completed 100% of that goal.

At the time, my goal was graduating from college and there was nothing that was going to stop me. My daily schedule was school, weight room, practice, and commute home—back to Los Angeles. One day, as soon as I got home from school there was yellow tape and neighbors standing around in tears. One of my neighbors described hearing gunshots, screeching tires, and a constant car horn. When he rushed outside, he saw my mentor in his car hunched over, with his head resting on the horn of car.

My friend, my mentor, and big brother, had been sitting in his car that morning after dropping his son off at preschool. A perpetrator pulled alongside of his car, opened fire on him, and pulled off. I was devastated when I found out that he had passed away because he did not bang. He trained me on the punching bag, and referred to me as his protégé. He made sure I did not bang, kept me updated on the latest fashions, and we always cracked jokes on each other. The loss of my big bro literally hit home for me, and I contemplated dropping out of college. That night I had a serious talk with my Pops, as he urged me to use college to get away from South Central L.A.

Football kept me focused and motivated to get a scholarship. My freshman year of college had come to an end, and during the off-season,

I started working as a soft coat security guard for red carpet events at the Kodak Theatre in Hollywood. I was making so much money as a security guard that I contemplated quitting football to work full-time and attend school. However, one of my teammates who worked with me convinced me not to quit football and assured me that our sophomore year would be our breakout season. He was from New Jersey, and we bonded well because we were both in the same predicament, as far as getting minimum playing time on the field. I believed him because it reminded me of high school, and how I did not get much playing time during my first season as a freshman on the field but ended up as a starter during my senior year.

SOPHOMORE

In 2004, I was the man off the field because I had a fast car, street ties, and was in college, which attracted more women than I could handle. I would take a different set of teammates to local house parties in South Central L.A. damn near every weekend. Football became an afterthought as partying and dating women became my main objective. Playing women had become a sport for me and by nature I was determined to be the best at it. Due to my decent grades, I was able to get an academic-athletic scholarship to Allen University in South Carolina.

THE EPIPHAY AT THE HBCU

In 2005, my teammate at PCC, who was from Jersey, received the same offer as me, and we were both on our way to South Carolina. This was my first time moving out of Los Angeles and being away from my family. It was a culture shock, but I was eager to make it work.

Allen University's football program was new, but its football field and locker room were used. My friend from Jersey was immediately turned off, as cockroaches roamed our dorm room. As for me, I was unbothered and excited to be away from South Central L.A.

Within the first week of being there, my friend had had enough and shared his epiphany with me. He said, "Man, God told me that we are not supposed to be here and there is somewhere better for us to play football. I feel it in my heart yo, we gotta go! Bro, I cannot take those big ass flying cockroaches anymore, I am out of here. I am going to play football at this college in Kansas named University of Saint Mary, and you need to come with me. We are better than this and need to play for a more established program."

The college in Kansas he was referring to was an National Association of Intercollegiate Athletics (NAIA) program in the middle of nowhere, and I had never even heard of an NAIA division football, but I did not want to be in South Carolina alone, so I opted to leave with him.

We flew into the Kansas City airport and traveled to Leavenworth, Kansas, to a small Catholic school named University of Saint Mary. Unlike Allen University, they offered us a partial scholarship and suggested we take out student loans to cover the remaining cost of the tuition.

I felt deflated because I knew I was worth a full scholarship, so I decided to return home, quit football, get a job, find a woman, and get my own place.

COLLEGE DROPOUT

As soon as I got back home from Kansas, I started hanging out more, attending street takeovers, and chasing women. One of my friends bought a Z28 Chevy Camaro too, and all we did was race. One day we were at a red light, side by side, revving our engines, waiting for the light to turn green. As soon as the light turned green, we burned rubber, accelerating through the light when suddenly there was sirens, sheriffs, and a helicopter hovering over us—as the cops commanded us to pull over. We did not even get to make it past the first block before getting arrested and booked for reckless driving.

I was embarrassed and ashamed.

I had dropped out of college and went to jail for a few days for reckless driving. This was the second time in my life being arrested, which had to be disclosed on all job applications.

During that fall, after spending a few days in prison, I had received a phone call from my friend from New Jersey, who stayed and played football at the University of Saint Mary.

He had played a season there and convinced me that the conference was easy and that we were going to get some playing time on the field. He said, "Man you should come back and enroll in the spring and play football next season. I am going to have the coach call you and make it happen."

I could not wait to receive that call from the coach to get out of L.A. because my life was headed in the wrong direction. I got the call, and that time around, I took the partial scholarship, took out some student loans, and headed back to Kansas for the beginning of the Spring semester in January.

UNIVERSITY OF SAINT MARY

It was January 2006, and I was living off campus with a few teammates who were heading into their senior season at the University of Saint Mary. It was a complete culture shock for me, coming from a big city like Los Angeles and moving to a small town like Leavenworth. The people were down-to-earth and equally weird, like their weather. The sky would randomly turn green and purple right before a thunderstorm during the Spring as it transitioned to the summertime, and it would be sunny minutes later. The clouds were close and down to the earth in the summer, as if Leavenworth was sitting on a hill. The sun was scorching hot as it hovered right over us, making it feel muggy and humid outside like a swamp. During the fall, the leaves would turn red, orange, and yellow then fall off right before the wintertime. In the wintertime the temperature would sometimes drop below zero, freezing anything outside for too long. I really enjoyed experiencing all four seasons. It was nothing that I could experience back home, where it was sunny 90% of the time and bugs at night and early mornings made noises that barked louder than dogs.

Everything was conveniently within miles of each other. There seemed to be one of everything in this town, one Walmart, one gas station, one bank, and one bar. There were little to no females that I was attracted to on and off campus, which kept me focused and out of trouble.

My buddy, who talked me into coming here, made the transition easily as he showed me the ropes around the school. There were roughly 600 undergraduates enrolled at the University of Saint Mary, but on campus, there were like 200 at a time and most of them lived on campus, so we saw each other all the time. The student body was mostly made up of athletes living on campus from all over the world. The classroom size was small, with roughly 10-15 students per class, which made it easier to get exposed during lesson and lecture time. I got exposed a few times for silly stuff like not knowing the difference between debt and depth and arguing with the class about it, but they understood me.

I finally declared my major — Business Administration—with an emphasis in marketing because that is what my older sister had chosen as her major at the University of Notre Dame. I was able to transfer most of my credits from Pasadena City College to the University of Saint Mary, which made me a junior in the classroom, with approximately four semesters left to graduate from college.

Miraculously, they did not count against me one of my playing years from the junior college I attended at PCC, and it gave me another year of eligibility for football. I had the eligibility to play three more collegiate football seasons if I wanted to. So, I was a junior in the classroom and a sophomore on the field.

My first semester there was during spring football and training. During spring ball, we had to practice twice a day, once in the morning and again in the evening, with school crammed somewhere in the middle. Our schedule was demanding as we had mandatory practice beginning at 4 a.m., Monday through Friday, which consisted of running around ten different stations from abdominal workouts to strength and conditioning circuits. As roommates, we watched each other pop up out of a deep sleep at like 3:30 a.m., just to sit-up and stare at the wall for long minutes, mentally preparing for what was to come. That was followed by practice followed by a long morning lecture. I dreaded coming in that early because it was midnight back in L.A. and we had to wake extra early for travel time. Some of us roamed into practice like zombies while others remained stuck in the bed starring at the wall. We competed against each other every day, and it prepared us for the upcoming football season. Spring training was mentally and physically tough but somehow, we became programmed and got used to the conditioning. It was a pivotal moment in all our lives as we were literally sharing college experiences, bonding, and preparing ourselves for the upcoming season.

Once spring ball was over, we continued the program throughout the summer. I stayed at school and transitioned from living off campus to moving on campus in my own dorm room.

We were headed into the summertime, and I continued to carpool to class and practice every day, until I was able to move into a dorm on campus over the summer. On campus as a team, we ate together, cracked jokes on each other, poured into each other, and partied together, eventually, forged a brotherhood between us. We spoke about opportunities that were to come on the field and how we were ready to win the conference championship.

Once I moved onto campus, life was much easier, I was able to walk from my dorm room to class, the cafeteria, and practice without depending on a ride. It was my first time living on my own without the aid of anyone, especially my parents.

I particularly remember the beginning of the fall semester which meant that the football season was finally here. As a sophomore on the field, I did not get much playing time due to not studying film and giving the other seniors their time to shine, but I was in on every special team making plays. It did not matter to me because once I knew that I was a junior in class with enough credits to graduate a year from now, that shifted my focus from playing football to getting a diploma. Up until this point in my life, I had no idea what I wanted to do for a living after college, but I knew graduation was approaching sooner rather than later.

Once the season was over, I traveled back home during the holiday break and stayed out of the way.

It wasn't long after that I returned to school for the winter/spring semester and decided to get a roommate to cut the cost of living on my own in half. My roommate happened to be the starting quarterback on the team from Detroit, Michigan. He was a natural-born leader and he showed me the ropes.

We trained every day, helped each other on and off the field, and quickly became more like brothers. We constantly challenged each other on almost every topic of discussion but never fought. It was iron sharpening iron at its finest. We would break things down for each other, and put things in perspective, and we almost always agreed to disagree.

I must have gained 15 pounds of muscle mass working out with him over that Spring Semester because when I visited my childhood friend, who used to live in South Central L.A., where we met years ago in grade school at Saint Anselm, who was now living in Atlanta over spring break, he could not believe it was me. This was my first time visiting Atlanta as an adult, and I was able to soak up the Southern hospitality as we visited places like the Blue Flame, Onyx, Glady Knight's restaurant, and Atlanta's nightlife.

I needed that break because life back in Leavenworth was like being in prison with special privileges. Leavenworth is home to federal, military, and state prisons where high-profile criminals, such as Mike Vick, would spend their time. It felt like I was sent to that school to do time for all the bad stuff I had done back home, and when I never got caught. It was God's grace and mercy that landed me here instead of behind bars in a jail cell and I was grateful.

I had been here for two years, but it felt like twenty years in Leavenworth. The time here was dragging, and I could not wait to go back home to South Central L.A. for the summer.

I returned home for the summer in the best shape of my life.

I SEEN DEATH AROUND THE CORNER

It was 2007, I was mentally and physically in the best shape of my life and remained the same OG.

My family and friends were astonished over my physique and transformation. Of course, my chiseled body came with a fast pass to the ladies as I took full advantage of all the attention.

That summer in L.A., before my senior year in college was one of the best summers in my life. My mind was clear, I was one year away from graduating from college, and I was back at home with my Z28 Chevy Camaro.

Still, I had no idea what I wanted to do for a living after college and thought I had enough talent to be an NFL prospect.

During my breaks from school, I did not intern or apply for any entry-level positions because all I wanted to do was have fun and hangout. That entire summer back home before my senior year all l did was workout, date women, partied, and hit the beach. I was a chick magnet, and my family and friends took full advantage of that as they invited me to every party in town. With this being one of my last vacations before being out of school permanently and I wanted to take full advantage of it.

Everything was going well that summer until the unexpected happened. It was around the 4th of July and the streets was hot this one summer night. There were fireworks sounding off around the city and it was common to mistake fireworks for gunshots around this time of the year. Me and a few of the homies were hanging outside that night, killing time and discussing our plans to find some girls at this party we were heading to.

As we were getting ready to leave for the party, one of the local kids who was hanging with us asked if he could go with me. I told him he could and to make sure he gets permission from his Grandma. He lived around the corner from me, so he headed home to get permission in a grocery cart basket as his friend pushed him down the street. I laughed and thought to myself, I hope he will be able to get in because he was not even 21-years-old yet. A part of me did not want him to go because if he were not able to get in, I would have had to bring him all the way back home.

As we continued to hang out in the middle of the street, waiting for him to return, within seconds we heard some shots pop out in the same direction as the kid in the grocery cart. We all paused for a few seconds to debate if it was gunshots or fireworks before we headed around the corner to confirm what we suspected.

Once I got to the corner, I saw the kid that was being pushed in the grocery cart laying on his back, at the edge of the curb, just outside of the liquor store fighting for his life. I ran up to him, ready to render my aid. I could not see the gunshot wounds, but I could see the blood running down from behind him as he fought for his life.

I pulled out my cell phone, and called 9-1-1, and I knelt down beside him, looked him in his eyesk as I encouraged him to hold on because help was on the way.

He had trouble breathing, and I could not believe my eyes. He started staring into the sky and looking past me as if I was not even there. He moaned as his blood and his life slowly slipped away from him.

Others started pouring in to revive and comfort him. We all started praying for him until the ambulance arrived 15 minutes too late to save him.

I could not wrap my mind around what had just taken place

He was just laughing while being pushed down the street in a grocery cart having fun like the big kid that he was to now being pushed on a gurney right after losing his life.

This was the same liquor store where the kid mentioned in Chapter One, who lived on my street, was shot and killed. This corner store was a death trap. Trouble was always lurking, especially at this liquor store.

I remained traumatized for a long time because I could not forget the look in his eyes, right before he took his last breath.

I had seen death around the corner.

After that summer in Los Angeles, I returned to school in the fall with a chip on my shoulder and had a lot to prove to myself.

SENIOR YEAR

It was 2008, and I was a senior in the class but a junior on the field and I was focused that season because if I decided to graduate and not come back the following season, it could possibly be my last time ever playing organized football with shoulder pads and helmets. I had no contract offers from any professional teams and to my knowledge no scouts were looking at me, so I gave it my all.

I studied film on the opponents every week before games and gave it my all in every practice. At some point in time during that season, I became the starting cornerback on defense and immediately made an impact on the field. I had everything going on for myself. The coaches attempted to use me on both sides of the football, whether it was on offense, defense, and special teams, but I could not catch the ball. I would run before securing the ball, anticipating that I would somehow catch it once it touched my hands, but it would somehow slip out every time. It stopped bothering me, though, because now I knew why I only played well on defense and not on offense. I was starting on the field and had not even realized it because I stayed in the rotation. It did not occur to me yet until I found out that I lead the entire Kansas Collegiate Athletic Conference (KCAC) conference in pass break-ups that season. It wowed me because that was not even a goal of mine, but I was not surprised because I put in the work, so I expected some results. I remained poised and eagerly anticipated the next season to make an impact and contribute to the team again.

Overall, I was thankful to be one of the contributors and impact players. There was no "I" in this team and we put in too much work throughout the year not to make a play in the game once football season came back around. We literally had to wait nine months like a pregnant woman before another season arrived and I was getting impatient.

Right after that season, I decided to move off campus and into some nearby apartments with a few of my teammates. That changed things drastically.

WATTS UP

This was my first time living on my own and having to pay rent and utility bills. I did not mind paying rent because it was my last semester of college. My roommate had a car, so he would drive us back and forth to the campus and everywhere else.

Living off campus was more entertaining as we met women at local bars, the local Walmart, and via social networking. We watched music videos on BET to keep up with the latest songs and new artists. The artists from the South were dominating the music scene until a new West Coast artist appeared on BET out of nowhere.

I first noticed the Nickerson Gardens in the music video and realized this artist was from Watts; Califronia. I immediately felt a connection because Watts ran through my bloodline too. The artist represented the east side of South Central L.A., which was my side of town, so I became eager to connect with him. I wanted to contribute to the east side movement, but I was still in college having fun. This new West Coast artist embodied the spirit of Watts through his raspy delivery and prideful lyrical content. Just like the city of Watts, he was gutter, raw, and unapologetic. The east side is made up of mostly Hispanic and Black families who are full of culture and ego. It made me proud to see my hometown on BET and even more ready to get out of college and contribute to putting on for my city.

But for now, I was stuck in Leavenworth, soaking up the college experience and living on my own for the first time in my life. All we did was party and go to church. Kansas University is in Lawrence, which was about 20 minutes away from Leavenworth. One of my cousins that I grew up with in South Central was attending KU and she kept us posted on some of their upcoming parties. Whenever there were not a party in Lawrence we headed in the opposite direction to Kansas City, Missouri once we found out that it was 30 minutes in the opposite direction. One of our teammates was plugged in with a local church in Kansas City, Kansas so we attended the church and the clubs in Kansas City, Missouri faithfully. The pastor at Church in Kansas City, Kansas was from Los Angeles, and he kept our spirit and stomachs full.

Later, I found out that I had family who lived in Kansas City, Missouri and one of my cousins from there would drive me back and forth from Leavenworth to Kansas City every chance he could. I appreciated him for taking care of me because he was a stranger up until that point. Also, he had added to my college experience and gave me something to look forward to outside of Leavenworth as I had big decisions to make—was I going to graduate in the spring or stay to play in my senior season of football?

U AIN'T GOTTA BE IN JAIL TO BE DOING TIME

I had the opportunity to graduate the next spring year or take less classes to come back and play for my senior season. So, I had to weigh the pros and cons of staying or leaving. The pros of staying were getting scouts to notice me and eventually earning a paycheck as a professional athlete. The cons were taking out another student loan for one more semester. I was tired of going to school and ready for it to be over with. I had played nine years of organized football and was not interested in taking out another student loan to play another year of football. I had several reasons for wanting to graduate from college instead of staying to play another season of football.

I was ready to be done with school, I had been in school for the past 18 years of my life and wanted out. I thought about my ancestors who paid the price to put a brother like me in a position to get a college degree. I thought about my family, friends, and the homies back home who did not get this opportunity and wanted to graduate for them. I wanted to be one of the first males in my family to graduate from college and provide a different route than the norm. Lastly, although I enjoyed experiencing all four seasons in Kansas, I was homesick and ready to come back home. One of my roommates challenged me to stay in Kansas and get a job until I had a plan. So, I started putting in job applications all over Kansas and I received a few offers for salaried positions, but I was too determined to get back home to Los Angeles.

In 2008, it was graduation time, and my parents and siblings flew out to watch me cross the stage and accept my diploma. It was one of the happiest moments in all our lives. Who would have thought this day would come for a misunderstood young Black man out of South Central L.A. allowing him to come out of the gutter where having a college degree was foreign to many? I knew I was no better than anyone else, but I made a pact with myself to be a positive influence within my family and community. There was enough negativity going around, and I did not want to add to it. I was a product of my environment and was ready to change the narrative from negative to positive. I was far from perfect, but I wanted to establish myself as a successful businessman by creating legitimate business entities. I wanted to lead by example and practice what I preached but that was easier said than done. I held myself to a higher standard and refused to dumb down who I had become to make others feel comfortable around me. All I needed was a plan to prove to myself that earning a college degree was worth the student loans and it was time well spent. Deep down inside I knew that going to college out of state kept me out of trouble and out of the streets and I was headed back home to the streets. This time around, I was hoping to contribute to the people around me in a positive way and stay in my own lane but that was easier said than done.

My college experience consisted of working out, sleeping, eating, and school. As I said earlier, there were no women on campus that I was attracted to, and all the attractions were hours away outside of Leavenworth. I finally understood what one of my all-time favorite rap quotes meant by "U ain't gotta be in jail to be doing time," especially while living in Leavenworth.

More importantly, I realized that God had spared my life and things could have been worse for me, I could have been dead or in jail. All I had to offer Him was my life as a living sacrifice.

Overall, the college experience gave me friends that I can call family from all over the globe for the rest of my life.

CHAPTER FOUR

LIFE AFTER COLLEGE REALITY CHECK

It was 2008, and I was back home with a different mindset and approach but first, I had to unwind. I had spent the last 18 years of my life in school and wanted a break before entering the next stage of my life. I started partying and hanging out with four of my close friends from high school again. The five of us were all successful in our own way and wanted nothing but the best for each other.

One of my friends convinced me to apply for the L.A. County Sheriff's Department as a probation officer. It required a four-year college degree, which I now had, and I felt it would be a good way of reaching troubled youth. He explained the hiring process would take a few months, so I had time to relax.

So, I applied, studied, took the exam, and waited for the results. In the meantime, I started going out to clubs picking up where I left off from back in Kansas.

One night, while clubbing, I ran into that West Coast rap artist from Watts that I saw a few months ago on BET while I was still in Leavenworth at school.

We exchanged numbers and met up at a later day to discuss some business plans and ideas. I knew by working with this artist, an east side great and a marketing genius, would allow me the opportunity to establish myself as a businessman. So, with the assistance of my editor, who had previously worked for *Detroit Free Press*, we whipped up some proposals that garnered the rap artist some sponsorships and his own signature line of customized beach cruiser bikes.

Everything was starting to look good and the only thing missing was my girlfriend. So, I decided to connect with a twin flame that I dated in the past before I left L.A. to college in Leavenworth to complete what I thought was missing.

In 2009, I had it all figured out, I was going to have a career as a juvenile probation officer, do marketing on the side with this rap artist, and start a family with my twin flame.

Repayment of my student loans had kicked in and the economy was now in a recession which delayed the hiring process with the probation department, and I needed some income. A close friend of mine was able to get me hired as an after-school instructor, but that was short lived after a parent and I got into a confrontation, and I was immediately let go.

One day, my cousin popped up at my house and we started applying for jobs together. We decided to apply at Sears®, and they hired me as a cashier. I needed more income and benefits than what Sears® offered, so I eventually used my cash handling experience from Sears® and was hired at a bank as a teller.

Having secured some solid income, it was back to partying until the probation officer career started and the bike deal that I was working on with the rap artist came through.

One night, after making it home from the club, I received a call that one out of my four close friends had died in a motorcycle accident.

I rushed to the scene just to see half of his bike lodged into a vehicle and the other half in the middle of street. His body had been catapulted across the street as a vehicle pulled out in front of him.

That was crazy.

The five of us were just on the block, huddled up laughing at funny stories we shared every time we linked up.

He had just had a baby when I found out that my girl was pregnant. At the time, I was too immature to realize the type of support she required, and she was too scorned to care about that life, so she aborted the baby without my consent.

It hurt me when I found out but, in the same breath, she did me a favor by removing the hurt she possessed out of my life. The flame was finally put out, and it was time for me to start taking some accountability for my own actions. I started taking inventory of myself and I realized I had developed some bad habits over time, and it was time for me to get rid of them and become more intentional. I started going to church again and repenting to God for all my sins, especially for the hearts of the women I had broke. I wanted to purge myself from as much sin as possible and replace the bad habits with good habits. I decided to get baptized for the first time as an adult. For a while, I stopped cursing, littering, smoking, and reciting the lyrics to certain songs. I quit hanging around people who did not mean me any well, and fornicating until they were gone. I did some soul-searching and replaced those bad habits with reading, studying, driving in silence, praying, and going to church. I had come back home from college and was leading myself in the wrong direction. I did not realize that smoking weed was affecting my decision-making process, and it caused others around me to stumble.

In 2010, I wanted to stick to the plan that I made for myself when I graduated from college, which was to make a change in my community, and the change had to begin with me. I decided to turn my life around, walk that fine line with Christ, and stay in my lane.

I started working out again and was still waiting to hear back from the probation department so I could assist with making a change in the lives of incarcerated youth.

One day, after coming home from working out, I saw a close neighbor who was more of a brother standing outside. I have not spoken to him since coming back from college. As we stood outside at his gate, an unmarked car with tented windows pulled up swiftly. We both paused and stared at the car as the door opened and someone popped out with a gun pointed it at us. I immediately thought to run until I realized the shiny badge around his neck and his command to freeze. So, I stopped and followed his commands as he cuffed me, and other SWAT cars pulled up.

It was like a movie, and I was the main character. I heard a voice on his walkie say, "Yes that is the shooter."

I laughed to myself while attempting to keep a straight face, because, I was not worried at all.

The officer frisked me and said that the community was tired of us shooting up the place and that I was going to jail for a long time. He asked me where the gun was and what was I doing over there.

I told him I lived across the street, and he asked me if he could search my house or wait for a search warrant.

At this point, I was hoping they were not attempting to set me up and railroad me, but I had nothing to hide, so I let them search. I was thinking by complying he would find nothing and let me go.

I knew that I was innocent and after finding nothing, he still took me to the station and arrested me for attempted murder. After being interviewed by the detectives, passing the ballistic test, and multiple calls to the station by my mom, they released me, and I was a free man.

Once I got home, I finally had received the results from the exam with the probation department, and I had received a 98 out of 100 and placed in Band 1. The hiring process was still dragging along because of the recession but at least I was employed at the bank and finally progressing in the journey of maturity. I was becoming more intentional and a more responsible adult. In the mean time, my little cousin had moved in with us from St. Louis, Missouri, in hopes of a better lifestyle and I knew he was watching my every move. So, I made sure to get a job, stay in church, and keep him inspired.

INSPIRATION

In 2011, while working at the bank on Crenshaw, I met this pretty lady, and we immediately started dating. She had one kid, and I accepted the kid as if it was mine.

After a few months of dating and spending nights with her, I eventually moved in with her and things suddenly became stressful. Even though I was shacking, I was glad to now become a one-woman man. This was my first time living with a girlfriend and we were down for the roller coaster ride. We went through many ups and downs and unnecessary loops, eventually, we both were drained and ready for the ride to end.

Working at the bank and going to church were the only two places I found peace. I started praying more and asking God to change my situation and send me a sign when two brothers walked through my bank doors.

I could tell by what they wore they were from the Crenshaw area, since I was from the east side of South-Central L.A. One of the brothers came to my window, and he began to talk to me. He was inspirational to the entire neighborhood, the community, and soon the world. He gave me his business card and told me to pull up to his shop across the street.

I did not realize that my prayers were being answered until I went to church that Sunday. While taking notes, reading the Bible, and daydreaming as usual, I saw the image of what appeared to be the outline of a tree and its roots. Suddenly, I was disturbed from daydreaming, God had given me a word, and the lady behind me gently tapped my shoulder and she said, "God told me that you are going to have a clothing line."

I never fully turned around to see her face but that did not matter because I had received the word.

"A clothing line . . . God, what should I call it?"

It was 2012, I was still living in confusion with my girlfriend, when I realized she was scorned from her previous relationship with her son's father and taking her fury out on me. It was a very stressful time in my life, and shacking was not it.

I ended up getting fired from the bank and had no income. Every day, I went across the street to the store by her house to use their computers, fax machines, and printers to apply for jobs. I did everything I could to stay out of the house and away from her.

While I was out of the house, I realized a lot of people in the streets wearing self-inflicting designs that contributed to more confusion in our communities than anything else. What you see is what you get, and what I was seeing at the time was negative designs dominating the clothing market. In return the people were receiving negative results. So, I wanted to provide an alternative to the market and dispel the negative stereotypes that mainly our young people were buying into.

We needed something mature that represented being established in our God-given purpose while feeling bold, trend-setting, and confident. I realized clothing was not only used as a vehicle to push a message but also as a silent protest. Without verbally saying something, your outer appearance speaks for you. We all know that words are powerful, including the words on our clothes. Words will someday manifest themselves, therefore we should choose our words wisely.

One of my all-time favorite scriptures in life is, *"Life and death is in the power of the tongue."* Your tongue has the power and authority to confront a situation and turn it around for better or for worse by the words that are coming out of your mouth. I was aware of this scripture, but putting it into action was easier said than done, especially because things were not going in my favor. Still, I continued to travail with my positive affirmations even when matters seemed to be getting worse. I made sure to attend church on Sunday because I figured that if I could get up and go out everywhere else throughout the week, then I could at least get up and make it to church on Sunday. As I listened to the message that Sunday, the Apostle of the house told us to turn to the Book of Romans in the Bible. As I scrabbled through Romans, there was one word that stood out to me, and as the Apostle began to break down the message, I began to daydream and saw a tree trunk with some distinct branches coming out of the bottom of the trunk. I closed my eyes tightly to reset my vision, and the same image of the tree trunk appeared in my eyelids in vibrant colors. For a second, I was amazed, but I immediately knew that God was attempting to tell me something, but I had not quite figured it out yet. However, I had put two and two together as the last word that I saw in the Bible before I started daydreaming was "Rooted."

After church, I called my baby sister to share the vision with her that I had in church. She confirmed that God wants us to start a clothing line and to name it "Rooted." The last thing I was thinking about was starting a clothing line because I had no experience, no interest in fashion, and no start-up capital to invest. On top of that, I had no designs and did not know where to start. The only thing I had was a message from God and I knew I had to deliver it.

I called a buddy who was into fashion and told him about the vision of the clothing line. We met up, and he sketched up some concepts on the spot. I showed everyone who was interested in seeing the mock-ups but still I had no logo for the "Rooted" name for the clothing line. My baby sister was always creative, and as I explained the vision to her, she helped me confirm the name—*Rooted Society.*

I contacted another close friend of the family who was in fashion, and she asked me to send her my concepts. I went back across the street, to the store by my girl's house, to fax over the concepts. The young store clerk complimented the designs. He told me he knew someone who was into graphic designing and creating logos. We immediately linked up, and I explained the clothing concept, and days later *Rooted Society* logo was conceived. Also, I shared the *Rooted Society* logo and concept with my little cousin who had moved in with us from St. Louis who was now a father and living with his girlfriend. We found ourselves in similar situations by being in toxic relationships, unemployed, and living with our girlfriends while trying to figure out life as we knew it. The only difference was, he had a second baby on the way. He was excited about the concept of *Rooted Society* and shared his ideas for the clothing line. It was hard to implement any ideas without cash flow and real-life struggles in our personal lives.

During this time, I had no income, my car had broken down, and I was still involved in a toxic relationship. Although the relationship was toxic, she worked with me, and helped me find a as-needed position with the city on Indeed website.

I immediately applied for the as-needed position, took the test, and waited for the results. In the meantime, I caught the bus to the fashion district that the brothers from Crenshaw told me about and looked for someone who could screen print my logo on some t-shirts at a reasonable price. Everyone's prices were high especially when you do not have the money or credit to pay for it.

Then, one day, while walking to my pop's house, I spotted a printing machine in a storefront and immediately got excited. I asked the people in the shop if they could print some t-shirts for me on consignment, and to my surprise, they agreed. Before you know it, they taught me how to use the printing machine and I started screen printing t-shirts on my own.

I linked up with a young videographer who I met while working with the rap artist from Watts, and we made a video to advertise and promote the line via social media. As people from all over started to support us, they equally complained about the quality.

I was not a fashion designer and was only looking to spread the message behind the name of the line. I needed a team such as a designer, office space, manufacturers, etc. The problem was I had no money, no income, and no business plan, but I did have a ton of support from family and friends who believed in me.

My plan was to work for the L.A. County Sheriff's Department as a probation officer while starting my own marketing firm and getting the clothing line to the masses. I also planned to find a wife, start a family, serve God, and live happily ever after. The reality check was that I thought I had it all figured out, but God had different plans for my life.

CHAPTER FIVE

WALK BY FAITH AND NOT BY SIGHT

In 2013, although I had a plan for my life and was eager to execute it, my reality was setting in, and I started to feel depressed. I was looking from the outside in and did not realize it. I had been out of college for five years at that time, and I was unemployed, no car, no money, with student loans, bills, and still involved in a toxic relationship, and virtually homeless—if it wasn't for my Pops. I felt the pressure of my reality weighing me down like an anchor on a boat. Feeling pressure was nothing new to me and it brought the best out of me. Feeling pressure was second nature for a Black man growing up in the ghetto but this pressure was different. I knew how to deal with pressure from the streets but the pressure from corporations by being ostracized from employment was different. I continued to remind myself that pressure burst pipes or made diamonds. I was still breathing and in my right state of mind and felt the love from some of the people around me, so I started to fight for my life. I became determined to make a diamond.

I reversed the curse by reminding myself of the definition of insanity, which is doing the same thing repeatedly and expecting different results.

So, I made a conscious effort to do things differently. I stopped littering, cursing, listening to secular music, and hanging around bad influences. This honest effort to do things differently, came with its own set of challenges but those challenges did not matter to me because I was already feeling low, so I had nothing to lose. I had mastered surviving, and it was now time to live.

I knew for me to attract the lifestyle that I envisioned I had to set some standards and hold myself accountable to it. I became more intentional and held myself to a higher standard. I had come too far from where I began to allow my current circumstances to stop me from progressing. Also, my parents had put too much unconditional love into me for me not to flourish, so I owed it to them and myself to turn this negative into a positive and become a diamond.

There was no doubt in my mind that I would need some Divine Intervention to make a diamond. So, I reinforced my efforts to stay in my own lane and out of the way from negative influences. I would mind my business and stay out of other people's business even if I got an open invite to entertain it. My Pops had a saying that resonated with me every time gossipers would come around with more bad news, "Mind your own, and you live long."

I took that saying to heart and applied in every applicable situation. My response to the gossipers was, "Nobody is perfect," or, "We all fall short of the glory of God."

During my time of unemployment, I was back it and forth living between my girl's house and with my Pop's house. Pops and I grew closer during this time, and we were thick as thieves. We had a lot in common, and we would find ourselves in the same place at the same time, and in the same situation. Work was slow for him and he was looking for something else to do that was less taxing on his body. He had retired from doing construction work and started to explore other hobbies, such as cooking and standup comedy. My Pops was a comedian at heart and loved making people laugh. He had no filter and would make a joke about any and every situation imaginable. We laughed and joked all the time, especially out in public. My Pops would call it like it is but in a joking manner and had code names for everything in sight. Before I knew it, everyone else who was around us would start laughing, too, as if they knew what my pops and I were talking about. He knew laughing was contagious and it could turn a frown into a smile. He often said that he missed his calling and should have been a comedian. He was not lying because he would keep going until it made you laugh, even if it was not funny. Sometimes, I would have to hold my laugher in because some stuff was embarrassing, but he did not care. When he saw me holding in my laughter, he would go harder until it forced me to crack up. I have enough stories that will have me laughing for a lifetime.

Whenever he shared a serious story with me and told me what his reaction or response to someone involved in the story, I would laugh because he did some questionable stuff but was dead serious, and I could not believe it.

I would call him Fred Sanford, from the TV show, "Sanford and Son," and he would reply, "And you're Lamont . . . you big dummy," in his Fred Sanford voice, followed by his laugh.

At the time, I did not know that Lamont was Fred Sanford's son until later in life. Now I know why he would laugh harder than me because he knew I had no idea that Lamont was Fred Sanford's son.

Every time we linked up, it was a celebration. We had inside jargon for every situation, and our body language was similar, so we knew what each other was thinking without even speaking.

He knew how to lift people's spirits with some words of encouragement and his infectious smile. We went to church together and one day decided to do some evangelist work by going to witness to people in the streets off

Slauson and Western. Initially, I had my reservations because that was not my style, but I said yes because I knew it would make him happy. We kept it simple while evangelizing, and whoever acknowledged us, we would simply say, "Jesus loves you!"

He knew I did not want no part of street witnessing in that manner, plus my ministry work was getting done through *Rooted Society*.

We checked off almost every father and son moment that I could think of. The only one we did not check off was him seeing me making him a grandfather. He was okay with that because he didn't want me having a kid out of wedlock, and he was already a Grandpa.

His firstborn, my oldest sister, had given him his first grandchild and my baby sister had given him his first live-in grandbaby, and he was crazy about her. My niece happened to be the firstborn grandchild on both sides of her family, so she was everyone's favorite baby. We often debated on who was the baby's favorite person in the house, and I would tell him that the baby's favorite people went in this order beginning with her nana, then me, then her parents, and ending with him. No shade to her parents, but she was a daughter-figure to me because she was born around the same time my aborted baby should have been born.

I treated my niece as if she was my own. She would crawl all the way to my room and stand up in the mirror screaming and watching herself until I grabbed her and held her while we chilled on my computer.

Pops said, "Bullshit, I'm her favorite person," and he had the story to prove it.

He reminded me of the time that we were all chilling in the living room on the long sectional couch, watching TV as a family. The baby was being held by her mother on one end of the sectional, and my Pops was sitting at the opposite end he called for the baby. From left to right, my Mom was sitting next to my Pops, then me. Next to me was my brother-in-law—the baby's father—and next to him was my sister holding her baby.

The baby literally climbed in and out of each of our arms, past her father, past me, past my Mom, and into my Pop's arms.

We were all astonished as he laughed at us all holding his grandbaby. I just knew I was her favorite right after her nana but somehow her poppa knew something that we all did not know and from that day forward there was no denying he was her favorite.

I was ready to make him a grandfather, but I had to get rid of my vices, find my wife, and establish myself as a man. I became very intentional when it came to dating and did not fornicate with anyone that I could not see myself spending the rest of my life with. I was done playing with feelings and breaking hearts. I wanted to purge myself from all soul-ties, lust, and bad habits, so I decided to get baptized as an adult.

Although, I was struggling in my personal life, God had given me Rooted Society.

THE MYSTERIOUS BLACK CAT

It was 2014, and I had moved back home and was finally over the toxic relationship with the woman and her child that I was living with. My focus was getting a job and figuring out a plan to spread the word about the clothing line, *Rooted Society*.

My younger cousin who had relocated from St. Louis, and was living with my parent's temporary, was one of the first people to witness the birth of *Rooted Society*. Every time we crossed paths at my parents' house, we would catch up, have deep conversations, and make plans for bettering our situations.

He eventually moved out and moved in with his girlfriend from high school. My younger cousin would assist me whenever he could, but by then, he had started a family, embraced fatherhood, and was raising two sons of his own.

We sort of lost touch with each other as we both were focused on getting jobs and dealing with life.

I had finally got a car and was looking forward to pulling up on him to catch up and to see his sons. The day that I decided to meet up with him was the same day my car alarm suddenly started going off while I was driving in traffic. I pulled up to a stereo shop, talked to a worker, and they disconnected the car alarm. As soon as I pulled off their lot, the car alarm began to sound off again. I was annoyed but kept it moving.

It was a late evening when I decided to go home that night instead of meeting my cousin to disconnect the battery and assess the problem. I pulled in the driveway, jumped out the car with the driver's door still left open, popped the hood open, and ran into the house to find some pliers to disconnect the battery.

After disconnecting the battery, I jumped back in the car and there was a mysterious black cat sitting in the passenger seat as if I invited him in. Me and the cat were both confused for a second because he wanted to get out, but the passenger door was closed, and I was in his way. I quickly jumped out to scare the cat out of the car as he scattered right across the driver's seat and out of the car.

After the cat was out of the car, he casually strutted next door, sat still under the neighbor's porch light until we made eye contact, and then he slowly walked toward the backyard before disappearing into the night.

I asked myself, What the heck was that about? I have never been superstitious, and I simply believed that everything happens for a reason. I had never had an encounter like that before but overall, I was unbothered. I eventually calmed my nerves, went into the house, and went to bed.

I forgot to turn my phone ringer off that night when my sleep was disturbed by a phone call around one in the morning. It was my baby sister, and she wasted no time telling me that our younger cousin was found dead at his girlfriend's house in a closet.

I quickly got dressed, hopped in the car, and rushed over to his girlfriend house. Some of my other family members were already there, and we did not believe the story that was told about how he went out. My cousin was literally a fighter, and he had two sons to live for, so in due time, the truth will come out. He was a kick-boxer and was training for a boxing match when his mysterious death took place.

I immediately knew what the mysterious black cat and the car alarm sounding off meant. It was God working in mysterious ways by alerting me that something was going on with my little cousin. I wish I would have pulled up on him before deciding to go home first. All I can do now is move forward in his memory and continue to push Rooted Society in honor of him. I was still unemployed and looking for a breakthrough.

NEW BASE

I had this God-given message in *Rooted Society* and needed some assistance in getting the message out to the masses.

One day, I was hanging out with my homies on the west side of town on 105th Avenue when I came across a local up-and-coming artist who handed me his mixtape. It was fire, to say the least, as he spoke about his experiences growing up in the streets of L.A. without any gang affiliations, which I found unique. We immediately connected as I recognized that he could blaze a beat and produce on his own. I introduced *Rooted Society* to him, and we immediately went to work and supported each other's movement.

He suggested we remove "society" from some of the gear and promote it as *"R.O.O.T.E.D."*

I agreed with him and decided R.O.O.T.ED. is an acronym that stands for Reigning Over Obstacles Throughout Each Day.

Everything was starting to come together, but I was still missing the business plan and a job for income. I started applying everywhere and was passing tests left and right. I was on the waiting list to be an electrician in the union, a firefighter, a probation officer, and the "as-needed" position with the city.

C.H.O.I.C.E.S.

I had been out of college for five years by this time with not much to show for the time spent in school. Believe it or not, I had never read a book from cover to cover, I was not articulate, and I had a hard time defining certain words that were used in our everyday language. Although I had a college education, I still felt illiterate, like an educated dummy. I had a business degree and wanted to go into business for myself, but I could not tell you how to start a business, how to scale a business, and how to read financial projections.

I knew to go into business for myself, I needed to study business models and learn the basics of Business 101. I was determined to become an entrepreneur, so I started going to the library reading business books, studying formulas, and how to apply them. I started watching business TV shows such as, *Shark Tank*, to get some understanding of basic concepts and some answers to my questions. However, watching it only made matters worse as they introduced new terms and formulas that I had never heard before in business such as valuations, perpetuity, and basic percentages.

I felt ashamed and behind as I started to blame the public school system in Los Angeles for my lack of real-world knowledge. The school system was known for passing kids along without properly preparing them for life outside of the school system also known as the "real world." For the most part, in the "real world" everything is based off credit and having a plan. I felt cheated out of life because I had no basic knowledge of credit, investing, and having a plan. I had no financial literacy and was left to figure things out on my own. So, I made an honest effort to educate myself and others who cared to listen. By teaching others what I had learned from reading and studying at the library allowed me to hone in on my wealth of business knowledge. I would compare and breakdown to them how attending six classes, for one hour per class in high school prepared us to become entrepreneurs. The logic behind my perspective was simple: whenever you go into business for yourself there are multiple jobs you must do to keep a business sustainable. For example, to run a successful clothing line, I needed to be able to do these six tasks consistently or the business would fail. I needed to design, order blanks, manufacture, promote, accounting, and distribute.

From my perspective this system was no different from any educational institution. So, I always encourage young people to at least graduate from high school, so if they ever go into business for themselves, they will be used to multitasking. Instead of making excuses for not being employed or making the most of my circumstances, I made a choice to change my perception of things. I stopped blaming the institutions that the government put in place to trap us or keep us dependent and reminded myself that we all have God-given *choices* or the freewill to do what we wanted.

Although, I was empathetic while speaking with others about their unfortunate circumstances due to this system that was created to keep us oppressed, I would not allow it to be an excuse. I would tell people at some point during our conversation now that we know better, we must do better and start making the right choices. Choices began to be a part of my everyday language and at some point, during this time, God gave me the acronym for *C.H.O.I.C.E.S.* which stands for Caring Hearts Outstanding Intelligence Committed to Educating Self. It was nothing more than another name for freewill.

A few years later, it was incorporated at the church I attended and is now the name of our mentorship program that is ran during the summertime to keep our young people busy from being victimized by idle time.

Everything was slowly but surely starting to come together.

CHAPTER SIX

GOD'S PLAN

The recession had been over for a few years now and around the same time I had contacted the city about the as-needed position, I received a letter in the mail from the Probation Department with an interview date.

To my surprise, the HR rep from the city told me that I had passed the exam, with the second-highest score out of the 400 candidates who had tested, and was placed in Band 1. The next step was background check followed by an interview and a start date. I had two jobs lined up, one with the city for the as-needed position and the other with the L.A. County Sheriff's Probation Department as a probation officer and was willing to go with whoever hired me first.

As I waited to hear back from the city, I attended an interview with the Probation Department and made it to the second round of the hiring process, which was background check. At the same time, as I was going through background check with the Probation Department, I had received a call back from the HR department at the city for the as-needed position with some bad news. They informed me that I was disqualified from the hiring process because I failed to list all my arrests on the application and that they were moving on to the next candidate.

I pleaded with the HR rep to give me a day to show them proof that the arrest that was not listed was expunged, which meant I did not have to disclose the arrest on the application.

As soon as I hung up the phone with the HR rep from the city, for the first time in my life, I laid face down on the living room floor with my arms and hands spread wide open in full submission, as if I was getting arrested, surrendering myself as I prayed to God. I said, "Dear God, show me where you want me to go. I submit myself 100% to you and I am all yours, you are the driver, and I am the passenger. Wherever you say go, I will go. Whatever is meant for me, show me and I will go and never look back. In Your son, Jesus' name . . . Amen."

As soon after I was done praying, I got an immediate unction to go to the Inglewood Court building, which was around the corner from where we were living at the time, to retrieve an expungement letter from the judge as proof to give to the HR dept for employment with the city for the as-needed position.

Once I got to the court, I spoke with one of the clerks behind the glass and told her about my situation. She told me that I had to get a court date to see the judge, which could take weeks, or sit in court and wait in hopes that he would see me at the end of his current cases, which she doubted.

At that moment, I remember thinking about a passage that I had read in the book, **Think and Grow Rich**, where one of the characters in the book refused to be denied. I respectfully declined her options and politely counteroffered and asked her if she could speak to the judge on my behalf during recess in the chambers.

She paused, and looked at me as if I was crazy, but she knew I was dead serious, so she accepted my offer.

To my surprise, she came back with the expunged letter, and I immediately emailed it over to human resources.

The very next day, I received a call from the city's HR department, and they explained to me that by law they had to give me an opportunity to explain the arrest in writing for an additional review.

After submitting the letter of explanation, I received a call back from the HR department that same evening with an offer and start date for the Revenue Collections position with the city. At this point in my life, there were no way that I could deny that God was real and now I had this as confirmation to prove it.

It was now the end of 2014, and I was now employed with the city and had a primary source of income. However, I still needed a plan to launch *R.O.O.T.E.D.* I started praying to God asking him for a sign which He usually responded through vivid dreams.

IT WAS NOT A DREAM

As 2015, arrived, I had been working for the City for a few months, and things were finally starting to turn around for me.

I had a job but was always tired due to the early work schedule. One night, I had a tough time sleeping, so I closed my eyes and started praying until I dozed off. Suddenly, I could hear my conscience speaking, but my vision was fuzzy. There was nothing else in sight but white space as if I was stuck in a cloud, and I could hear my conscience's voice pleading for answers to my questions . . . *Where am I? What is going on with me? Where is my body? Where is everybody at?*

My conscience voice got quiet for a second, as I forced myself to remember my last fond memory. I remember seeing sparks, and that I was in the ambulance, and that was it. I felt okay as if nothing had happened to me, but something was definitely different with me.

I began to beg God to at least allow me to see my Mom, as I felt stuck in this new state of existence.

Suddenly, I could see my Mom sitting still in the kitchen staring in space. I was directly in front of her, up close, yelling at her.

"Mom, I'm right here! I'm okay! Why are you ignoring me? Why are you looking like that? What is wrong with you? What is going on? Why is everyone here at the house?"

She never responded because she could not hear or see me. She was in a daze until someone offered her a piece of fried chicken. As I turned around to see who had offered her the chicken, my vision became cloudy again, and my consciousness dissipated into a peaceful place.

I woke up sweating and panicking for my life because I had realized God was going to take me away.

On my way to work I started asking God why me? What did I do to deserve to die so soon?

At some point during the drive to work, I accepted my soon-to-come fate and contemplated if I should share the dream to prepare my family for what was to come.

A few weeks had passed, and by then, I had forgotten about the dream. I drove down the street where my cousins used to live, in South Central L.A., while on my way to our family's favorite fish market. As I drove past their old building, I thought about the time when I was a kid running alongside the building. I had been pushed from behind by my older cousin, as we attempted to outrun a barking dog on the other side of the fence. I busted my head on the water meter, which required staples in my head, and I was never the same after that.

I had driven to this fish market hundreds of times and never gone down my cousin's old street before this and thought it was very random for me to be going down his street out of the blue. A few days later, I remember laying on the couch watching the kickoff to the new 2015 NFL season and just before dosing off, I got a notification from Facebook of my cousin recent post. I liked the post and went to bed.

The next morning, while at work, I received a call from my sister telling me that our cousin was deceased. This was the *same* cousin who lived on the street that I just rode down while on my way to the fish market.

We had so much in common that even our mothers seemed to resemble each other.

He was a special dude, had many talents and was an overall trailblazer. He had tried out for a few professional basketball teams and was given an offer by the Lakers' D-league squad team right before his tragedy.

He was gone too soon, but his legacy will forever inspire me.

A few days after his passing, I recalled the dream of my clouded conscious state of being and how I just knew that it was going to be me. But now I knew why I had gone down his street because God was attempting to tell me something.

I shared the dream with his parents a few days after his tragedy, but still, no one could have predicted that his passing was coming. This was a very unfair situation. We cannot wait until we learn what really happened on the night he died.

My cousin was a people's person, a ladies' man, with many gifts, so I could relate to the hate he received that night, and my focus shifted from selective dating to celibacy until marriage.

After the tragic death of my cousin, I did not want no parts of the streets because this was not a dream. It was a message.

RESTORED

In 2016, I was transformed by the renewing of my mind through the work I had put in to turn my life post college. I made a conscious effort to educate myself, abstain from fornicating, and grow closer to God.

For the first time in my life, I knew my true worth and refused to settle for less. I could have cared less about anyone's opinion, no matter if it was good or bad. I was sober and celibate for the first time in my life and it was the most potent I had ever felt. My plan was to remain celibate until marriage and never share my body with anyone else outside of my wife.

I was clicking on all cylinders—mentally, physically, and spiritually.

I got promoted at the city from as-needed to full-time permanent and was able to get my own place for the first time in my life.

I was ready to permanently settle down, so I began to search for a God-fearing woman who could match my capacity to serve God.

I thought I was ready to settle down because I had mastered being faithful to myself and self-discipline. I just knew this was the plan that God had for my life to find a God-fearing wife, start a family, work this 9-to-5 job, secure multiple sources of income, and live happily ever after.

I started noticing a young minister who I went to high school with preaching the word on my timeline every day when I logged onto Facebook, and I wanted to get to know her. We met at a bowling event she threw for her birthday, and after that day, I knew she was the one for me.

She was devoted to God like none other and was the first female friend to openly pray for me daily. We became good friends and before we knew it, we started dating.

This was the first time I had ever dated anyone without being physically intimate. We were determined to honor God by remaining abstinent until marriage. Although I had my days and moments where I attempted to give into temptation, she was not having it. I was okay with it because waiting for marriage was a goal of mine, and I was determined to achieve it. She checked off everything I envisioned in a lifetime partner, so I decided to propose to her. We had been dating and courting for about two years by that time, so I knew she would say yes.

I remember my car would not start on the day that I planned to propose to her, so I used Uber to get to the meet-up spot. I remember thinking to myself in the back seat of the Uber ride, like either the devil or God does not want us to get married. I had made up my mind that I was not going to allow anything to get in the way of our union.

During the proposal, my hand got stuck in my pocket as I tried to pull the ring out.

She noticed the struggle and giggled as I finally took it out. I popped the question, she said, yes, and we kissed as friends and family cheered us on.

The next step was premarital counseling, choosing a venue, and the wedding date. During our premarital counseling stages, a few red flags surfaced, but we both felt like we could work through them.

Choosing a venue was tough due to the overcharge, but we knew that was a part of the process as we finally agreed to get married off the water in Long Beach.

It was 2018 when, wedding day finally arrived. I had dealt with adversity my whole life and was willing to overcome whatever obstacle may arrive during our marriage.

A few months after getting married, my Pops got sick, and his life was permanently altered as I was experiencing two life-changing events at the same time. I was a newlywed adjusting to a new lifestyle and at the same time, I now had to care for my Pops. It was an honor to take care of him because he had taken care of me my whole life, so this was the least I could do. My Pops had as much support and resources as possible, but I could tell he was unhappy because he had lost his independence.

It hurt me so much because I was optimistic about his recovery, and he made an honest attempt to recover, but it did not happen fast enough for him. He was growing impatient with the recovery process and some of the company around him made matters worse.

We decided, as a family, to convince my Pops to temporarily move out of state and live with my older sister, who was a stay-at-home mom at that time, to recovery and focus on his health. But he refused to leave home.

At the same time, after a year of being married, my marriage started to unravel as we sought therapy and outside support.

Marriage will expose all your stuff at some point in time. You may not realize that you are hurting, but your spouse will feel your pain. Those words that the preacher conveys at the altar with you and your spouse are as real as the Bible version of two becoming one.

I had unpacked childhood trauma that started to surface and did not realize it until I was married. Growing up, I did not believe in seeing a therapist, so things were unknown. The way we dealt with trauma was internalizing it, turning to sex and drugs, instead of having a professional or someone to vent and help process things. Being numb to my feelings became detrimental to my thought process, emotional intelligence, and ultimately, the marriage.

I realized that hurt people hurt people. So, I finally decided to get some therapy for the first time in my life.

CHAPTER SEVEN

TO DEATH DO US PART

In 2019, during therapy, I got diagnosed and was able to put into terms the way I was feeling inside for all those years—trauma.

I was traumatized by the things I experienced growing up, especially hearing, and seeing my childhood friends lay stiff in caskets. For all those years I used sex and drugs to numb the pain, not realizing it was a temporary fix for what I was really harboring inside of me. I was a shell of my true self and had buried my feelings along with the family and friends I had lost over the course of my life. I took the first step which was admitting I had unpacked childhood trauma but unfortunately, I had unpacked it on my wife, and some stuff should have been addressed before I got married.

We decided to get a divorce toward in middle of 2020, and it was finalized at the end of 2021. It felt like I had lost one of my limbs, as I turned to familiar vices to numb the pain. I was already dealing with childhood trauma, and getting a divorce only added onto the trauma.

For the first time in my life, I was all alone, and to make matters worse, my Pops health had tremendously declined. His condition became worse as he lost full independence. He could not speak, and he needed around-the-clock care. During this time, he was in and out of the hospital, a nursing facility, and home. There were a lot of miscommunications between the family at the time, which caused more confusion, but some family member's actions were downright foul. This was the time for our family to come together and support my pops, by taking turns to take care of him, but none of us could get on one accord. I am not here to point a finger and blame anyone for their actions during the time my pops needed his family the most because it will not bring my pops back to life.

So, I choose to forgive them, myself, and love them from a distance.

On May 4, 2022, six months into wrapping my mind around the divorce, I was on my lunch hour and went to the gym, and in the middle of a workout when I received a random phone call from one of the pastors from my church and he started praying for me.

Right after the prayer call, I received another call from my mom. She told me my Pops had just passed away.

I left work and headed to the hospital hoping it was not true and hoping when he felt my presence, he would mysteriously wake up and come back to life like he always did when I saw him.

Once I got to the hospital, I spoke with the nurse who was with him during his last hour alive. I wanted to know what happened in detail because I had just saw him the night before and he was hanging in there.

After I spoke to the nurse, I slowly walked into the room where his body was lying. He was wrapped up in white cotton and linen sheets as if he was sleeping.

Each tear that rolled down my cheek symbolized a different feeling. I felt this unexplainable out-of-body experience as if we had switched places. I believed his presence was still in the room as I prayed over his body, and I felt this instant comfort.

I instinctively drew nearer, removed the towel from over his mouth and put my hands on his forehead, waiting for him to respond.

There was no response, of course, and I knew there was nothing I could do to make him come back alive.

He was at peace, and I thanked him for all the lessons and experiences.

Internally, I could still hear his voice providing me with instructions and comfort as I left the room as a newfound man.

The only person who could mend my heart was my Mom because she was the only parent I had left.

I felt broken and needed some intervention to ease the pain.

Feeling depressed was an understatement as I turned to sex, weed, and therapy to help me cope with the trauma that I was experiencing, but that seemed to make matters worse. Although consented sex seemed to be a temporary stress reliever, it came with lust and soul ties that lasted longer than the temporary time of pleasure.

Once I sobered up from smoking, the trauma I felt before smoking was still hanging around like a bad habit. We all need someone to vent to, but some therapists seemed to send me back down into the quicksand because of the lack of connection.

I was at a crossroads in my life, and reading and writing became the intervention that I needed, so I began reading the Bible and writing about the stories I read which gave me a different perspective on life. It was therapeutic, and it brought the best out of me.

Although I still felt pain, I knew my Pops would want me to hang in there and continue to finish what he started. My focus was taking it one day at a time as I eagerly looked forward to getting out of the year with no more heartbreaks.

On October 31, 2022, five months after my father passed away, I received a phone call from my mom and this time her brother, my uncle, one of my Pop's caregivers, had passed away in his sleep overnight. My uncle was dear to my heart for a few reasons, but mainly because he was one of the only family members who moved in with my Pops to help take care of him during his time of need and now, he was gone, too.

I rushed to the house where he was located, hoping to see him before the ambulance hauled his body away, but it was too late.

I said a prayer for his salvation and comforted my other family members who lived there with him. My grandmother was living in this house as well, so, I went to her room to comfort her, but she was fast asleep. I stood over her and contemplated waking her up, but she was resting in peace. So, I kissed her forehead, and I saw her eyeballs move underneath her eyelids.

The following morning, on November 1, 2022, I received another phone call from my mom to tell me that her mother, my grandmother had also passed away. I was already heartbroken and still processing the loss of my father, then my uncle, and now my grandmother. I would cry sometimes, but for the most part, the pain and agony always harbored inside. I immediately thought about my grandpa because he was the only grandparent I had left. We were already close and spoke on a weekly basis but now I needed him more than ever.

ON AUTOPILOT

At this point, I was a complete shell of myself. The lights were on, but nobody was home.

I walked around on autopilot. What I mean by that is, I was physically present doing my daily routine, like going to work but mentally, my mind was in another place. I was still in shock over the loss of my pops and now I had to live without one of my favorite uncles and beloved grandmother. I was in a daze and going through the motions at this time in my life, processing the hurt and pain I felt from multiple back-to-back-to-back fatal losses that pierced my heart. I would sleep all day and was not in the mood for anything or anybody. You would think that experiencing back-to-back-to-back-to back losses from the finalized divorce at the end of 2021, to my pops passing five months later on May 4, 2022, to my uncle passing six months later on October 31, 2022, and finally my Grandma passing away the very next morning on November 1, 2022, would be enough to drive a man insane but then the unthinkable happened.

In December of 2022, a month after my uncle and grandmother's memorial service, while still lying in bed that morning, I received a phone call from my older sister, who was in town visiting and staying with our mother. She told me that our Mom had fallen and could not get herself up, so my sister called the ambulance right away. The paramedics came within minutes and took her to the nearby hospital for an immediate procedure. My Mom was at the hospital, and my sister could not be by her side at the hospital because she had her baby with her. My breath was instantly taken away as I laid in the bed sobbing and fighting for my sanity. First, my Pops, had passed, then my uncle, followed by my grandmother, and now my mom was in the operating room all in the same year. I could not believe what was happening, my life had changed in the blink of an eye. The thought of losing two parents in the same year was looming over my head.

I jumped out of bed immediately and instinctively started praying while getting dressed to go be by my Mom's side to comfort and pray for her during her time of need. I was so distraught that I could not cry and could only react. I knew this was not the time for crying but a time to rely on my faith and prayers.

Once I made it to the hospital, I found the room my mom was in and made sure the doctors told her I was there as I watched her every move through the glass window in the door.

I remained in the hallway, praying earnestly while the medical staff prepared to move Mom for surgery. Once she entered the hallway to get transported to the surgery room, I made sure she saw my face and could hear my voice. I kissed her, told her not to worry, and that I would be here praying for her until she made it out safely.

Eventually, I calmed myself down, and I went to the waiting room. I sat down and held onto my baby niece as her innocence comforted my sorrow.

The procedure went well, she recovered, and my Mom was finally able to leave the hospital. I was thankful my sister was in town, staying with my mom at her place when this happened because it could have been worse.

Once I got home, I cried out to God and asked Him what He wanted from me.

At this point in my life, I felt like a failure and needed some reassurance.

CHAPTER EIGHT

THE TIES THAT BIND

It was 2023 and, although, I was living a decent lifestyle and able to afford to live on my own near the beach, I still felt like a failure and was fighting for my sanity. My marriage failed in 2021, I lost my father, grandma, uncle, and nearly my mother in 2022. I had no family of my own, and I was lonely.

I failed to give my father a grandbaby before he passed away, and I felt alone even when I had company around me. My mom was recovering but I could still feel her pain. I had just buried three family members who were near and dear and close to my heart.

In my personal life, I felt like I had neglected the clothing line, due to personal reasons, and I was working a 9-to-5 job that did not care about what I was going through. It was not their fault because I failed myself by not fully living up to my potential and the expectations I had set for myself.

I did not want to be a burden on anyone else around me, so I isolated myself and stayed away from family and friends. I felt like no one could relate to the pain I was feeling inside. My siblings had families of their own and were grieving in their own way, so I refrained from reaching out to them because I did not want to disturb their peace. Some close friends and family would reach out from time to time to check in on me, but they constantly reminded me of the agony and pain that I was trying to escape by bringing up memories of my pops, so I started to avoid their phone calls.

I was all alone and felt like God had abandoned me and was mad at me for the things I had done wrong in my past. God finally had me to Himself and as I started to reflect on my life and current circumstances, I had questions for Him.

Who am I? What is my purpose? What is my gift to the world? What did God want from me? Why was I suffering so much when I gave myself to You?

As I continued to reflect on my life, I thought about the fumble experience that took place after the interception I made way back in high school, which is mentioned back in Chapter 2. My life at that moment reminded me of that promising touchdown that was right in front of me right before I mysteriously fumbled the football. I was having an identity crisis. I had fumbled my marriage and felt like I was losing control of my life. I knew I had come a long way from where I started, but I also knew God did not bring me this far just to fail me.

Although, I had a lot to be thankful for, this was not the life that I envisioned for myself, especially after reading about the miracles God had performed for the people He chose in the Bible and the ones who had submitted themselves to Him. I had questions I needed answers to. I was mentally, physically, and spiritually in a very deep, dark place in my life, and the only other way was to go up. I began to fight for my life by reading the Bible, listening to Gospel rap, and writing out my feelings. I knew that God himself was the only source who could pull me out of this hole, so I became determined to hear from Him. Out of innocence, I continued to question my purpose.

What about the covenant we as believers have with You? Was I apart of this covenant or not? Why are we suffering so much? Are you mad at us? What do You need from me? Here I am, Lord, use me. I was desperate for some answers and demanded to hear back from God.

There was no insight and no one to vent to and all I could do was vent to God and repent. I was determined to make some sense of my situation and life in general.

I started cleaning up my place, and I came across a 3-ring binder that I created years ago, right after I graduated from college I had forgotten about, that I used as a portfolio of myself to show off to future employers. In this 3-ring binder, I saved all my academic, athletic, and personal achievements from high school up that time. Inside the 3-ring binder was a picture of me being baptized as an adult, along with test results from the Probation Department with a score of 98 out of 100 (I literally missed one question) from a 150-question test that I had taken to become a probation officer right after college. My college transcripts and college diploma, mock-ups for my *Rooted Society* clothing line, my high school diploma, and an article of me from the L.A. Times newspaper for football during high school.

This 3-ring binder held the essence of my true self, and it reminded me of who I really am despite my current circumstances.

I immediately started praising God for answering my prayers and reminding me who He created me to be: consistent, an overachieving, competitive, faithful, and chosen human being. These achievements were a reminder that God had been using me this whole time, and I was too blind to realize it. At the same time I realized that my plan was not the same plan God had for my life.

I began to praise God and be more thankful for the small finite things we as humans can sometimes take for granted such as the ability to breathe, and wake up every day in our right state of mind with the ability to utilize all of our senses, and bodily functions. Although some of my close loved ones were gone, I was still alive, and God was not done with me yet. I continued reading Bible stories, and it reminded me that my story was still being written. The stuff in this 3-ring binder was there to remind me that I was not a failure, and they became a symbol of the ties that binds me.

Amid venting, I continued to read the Bible and take notes, and as I continued to read the Bible, I noticed a pattern and some similarities that were consistent with what I was experiencing in my personal life and what I had found in the binder. God had separated the ones He chose to complete a particular assignment that He was preparing for them. For example, God isolated Moses by calling him up into the mountains to write down the Ten Commandments and deliver them to the children of Israel. As I continued to read the Bible and take notes, I started to realize that God had been using me this whole time and there was no way I could deny it. I did not believe in giving myself credit for any of my personal accomplishments, because I put in the work, and I was doing what I was supposed to be doing, so I expected results. No matter if it was good or bad, I did things whole-heartedly and would put my all into everything I attempted, so I did my best to make sure my efforts went into things that would yield positive returns and represented God.

I started to understand God's plan for my life and how to play the cards that were dealt to me. I started to embrace my uniqueness and who God called me to be. I could not shy away from the truth, even if I tried to. It became my responsibility to lead the ones closest to me back to Christ through the gifts He had given me. I understood that I could lead you to the water, but I could not make them drink. I could only lead by example and let my actions speak louder than words. For example, I understood that if you seek God whole-heartedly, repent your sins, and commit your works to the Lord, He will use you for His glory.

By reading the Bible, I understood that He works in mysterious ways. He is so practical that it is easy to miss, and He will use anything and anyone for His purpose. Everything I went through good and bad was preparing me for the plan He has for my life. So, I started to embrace my journey, and I used my past trials and tribulations as experience and did my best not to repeat the same mistakes. I began to thank God for the hard times because it taught me coping skills, so I did my best not to complain but to embrace my journey.

Once I knew God was using me for His glory, I started aiming higher. The Bible says, judge a tree by its fruits, and based on the results from my previous work, I was doing alright for myself. I noticed a pattern of resilience and that there was nothing that I could not do, that would not yield high results. I wanted to make sure the fruits of my labor represented God's hands on my life. So, I never measured my success again because I was doing it out of obedience and not for the attention of others. I just did my best, aimed for perfection, and let the results speak for themselves. I knew there was nothing I could not do, based on the God I served, and the proof was in the Bible.

While reading the Bible, I became even more convinced that I had overcome all these trials and tribulations due to divine intervention. After all I had been through and survived in this short span of time and I was able to write about it and share it with others is a miracle within itself. There was no doubt in my mind that God had a bigger plan for my life that had yet to come.

Because history repeats itself, I could see God's hands on my life, and I knew that I was no different than the characters He had previously used in the Bible. Just like the other characters, I was grieving and frustrated with God about my life, my circumstances, and I demanded a miracle.

Although I had discovered something special about myself, I was still grieving and hurt inside. My appetite was off, I was not eating, and I was still processing the loss of my family members, especially my Pops.

Every day, there was something that would remind me of my Pops such as songs on the radio, conversations with people, movies, and jokes. I would be in public and laugh out loud because I could hear my Pops cracking a joke or doing something raunchy. I would see him in my dreams and have full-on conversations with him in my sleep, as if he were still alive. There have been several dreams where I could hear my Grandma's voice, calling my name, and of other family members that had both passed away and who were still alive. My dreams were so vivid that I would remain in a daze even after waking up. I know that the dead cannot cross the living and vice versa, but these dreams were lucid.

Although, I was isolated with no one to vent to, I would call my Mom and my sisters to share some of the lucid dreams, I had experienced, and to check-in on their well-being.

CHAPTER NINE

PEN CRY™

@PENCRYLA

Everyone grieves differently . . .

It was July 2023, and it had been a little over a year since our Pops left us. My siblings and I were always close, but the loss of my father brought us even closer. Over the past year, we found ourselves calling each other on a weekly basis to vent, share memories, to laugh, and to catch up. We realized how delicate life was and became more intentional by verbally expressing our love for one another. My baby sister was my Pop's favorite by default, because she was the baby in our immediate family, so I knew it was my job to console her the most.

I called my baby sister one day to check-in on her well-being but in all honesty, I needed her the most. I could tell she was more concerned for me than I was for her because I was living alone, and she knew me, and Pops had a close, strong bond. Plus I could not cry. No matter how hard I tried to cry or wanted to cry, I simply could not. The agony and pain would harbor inside until I could find an outlet. She must have felt my pain through the phone because I was boiling inside. I was still in disbelief and did not have a place to vent and process the loss I had experienced.

She encouraged me to seek therapy, but I had already tried to speak with a therapist, and it was helping a little bit because all I really needed was someone to vent to. But it was not sufficient. I needed more time to process the loss of my marriage, father, grandma, uncle, and nearly my Mom, but the 50-minute therapy sessions were inadequate. After each session, I felt more open and needed more closure, so I started writing, backtracking, and creating a timeline of events in an attempt to pinpoint and extract the pain that was boiling inside of my soul.

I told my baby sister that I had been writing, and it became therapeutic because I was able to express myself and go into details without any time constraints. Writing also became a creative outlet because it allowed me to get a lot of things off my chest and out in the atmosphere. Writing was the challenge that I needed because I was naturally a perfectionist and articulating a concise and compelling story in the form of a book kept me focused, and it eventually transformed the pain into comfort.

Every time I felt the need to express myself, I would write and not stop because writing became addictive. As I continued to explain this newfound outlet to express myself through writing to my sister, she began to relax and could relate. She was a writer herself and wrote lyrics to express herself.

Simply put, I told her that every time I felt grief and pain, I would let this pen cry.

She asked, "Where did you get that from?"

I replied, "Get what from?"

She said, "Pen cry."

I responded, "From the top of my head. It just flowed out like that." I explained to her that I had never been the type to cry, and I understood that everyone grieves differently. So, since it was hard for me to physically cry, I had to let the pen cry.

As days went on, I thought about that conversation I had with my baby sister and thought she was a genius for pointing out "pen cry."

My Pops always said that she was the most gifted and talented out of all his kids and at that point, I was a believer.

Being the entrepreneur that I am, I decided to trademark the words "Pen Cry" and use it in business as a writing/publishing company. I believe that there are more people who will find writing therapeutic and express themselves through different forms of literature via song, book, movie script, etc., and can maybe publish their works through "Pen Cry."

What we did not know was I had instinctively found my purpose, as I began to feel a great sense of release and purpose whenever I expressed myself through writing and storytelling to draw all men unto God.

CHAPTER TEN

THE COVENANT

THE BOW IN THE CLOUD . . .

The bow in the cloud is the token of the covenant God made with us. As I finished writing the last chapter of this book, I had just finished reading the book of Job and I could relate to his story the most. Like Job, I know that my later days will be better than my former ones.

After all that I had been through, from losing three close family members in 2022, being divorced in 2021, being and quarantine all in 2020, and overcoming traumatizing life-changing events, that will forever influence my perspective of life. There is no way one can still be sane or explain this mysterious journey without some Divine Intervention from God.

I felt like my life was always under a constant attack, until I started reading the Bible, starting with Genesis. I started recognizing how God works in mysterious ways. Even in my darkest hours, He sent signs and wonders to remind me that He's still got me. Through my trials and tribulations, I recognized that He was using me to draw all men unto Him. I would not have recognized how He operates if it was not for reading Bible stories like David slaying Goliath.

For example, before David defeated Goliath and became king, he had to slay a lion and a bear before they ate one of his father's sheep. This victory gave David the confidence and experience he needed to defeat Goliath.

I'm sure David had no idea that he was going to slay Goliath and become King David.

I doubt if David even cared to be a King, he just put all his trust and faith in the Lord, and put in the work with the sling that was in his hand. When David saw how tall Goliath was, I'm sure he had a flashback of defeating the bear that stood up 9 feet 9 inches tall on its hind legs, which was probably around the same height as Goliath.

David called on the Lord, while releasing a smooth stone right through the forehead of Goliath. All Goliath could do was fall on his face to the earth and die.

David slayed Goliath by putting God first, he called on the Lord before releasing that stone, and the rest is history. He was not afraid to take a shot!

My prayer is that we all learn how to put the Lord first, and release our faith into Him. David was a flawed human being, just like you and me, but God still used him. We are no different than King David. The story of how David slays Goliath is one of my all-time favorite stories in the Old Testament. In fact, we have somewhat of an advantage because we have this type of example or history to draw from, which is all in the Bible.

If none of this applies to you, just know that God's plans will always supersede yours, just keep living.

As you continue to read the Bible, beginning with Genesis, you will see that He is the same God back then and the same God right now. There is nothing new under the Sun and history will continue to repeat itself. We have a covenant with God, that He will never leave us nor forsake us, and He sends us the bow in the cloud as a reminder us of the covenant. And sometimes we miss the bow because we are too busy in our heads, instead of looking up to Him.

Our salvation with the Lord is true liberation, which money cannot buy, and no man can take from you.

All of this may sound, easier said than done, but it's been done before, and it will be done again. Be patient with the process. Life is a journey, full of ups and downs. So, embrace yourself and the process. Remember this, the cards that you were dealt such as: your gender, race, ethnicity, family members (biological or not), and even the circumstances you were born in are out of your control. So, at some point you will realize that you can only go so far without God.

Set some goals for yourself and embrace your journey and know that God has chosen you to be here alive in this present day in time for a reason or you would not be reading this book.

Ask and you shall receive. Be careful what you ask for because it may not align with the plans God has for your life. Ask Him what is the purpose for your life. I hope you use your gift to draw all men unto the Lord. Now it's your responsibility to figure it out and execute it in a civilize manner.

Lastly, the plans God have for your life will always supersede your plans. God works in mysterious ways. God is so practical that He is sometimes easy to miss. The only way to know Him is by studying the Living Word, which is the Bible. It's full of instructions and examples to living life.

Remember, we all have sinned, and come short of the Glory of God. Nobody is perfect, so give grace and mercy and it will be added to you. However, you reap what you sow, so do not take others' kindness for weakness. Put in the work and you will yield in due season. What you put in, is what you get out.

As you continue your journey in life pray for forgiveness, favor, discernment, and Divine Intervention.

ACKNOWLEDGMENTS

To God for choosing me to write. He is my rock.

To my parents for their unconditional love.

Pops, what's understood doesn't always have to be said.

To my Moms, for all those lectures, prayers, and our friendship—iron sharpens iron.

To my siblings for being my best friends, and to all my family members on both sides of my family, in-laws, friends, and church family—I love y'all.

To the people in the streets, hospitals, and prisons—KEEP YO HEAD UP!

And to whoever is reading this book, your salvation with the Lord is true Liberty!

R.I.P. to the ones who has gone before us.

Last but not least, to everyone who had a role in bringing this book to life, we will forever be a part of history!

#Frontline

ABOUT THE AUTHOR

Corey, hailing from the renowned South-Central L.A., has had his worldview and storytelling significantly influenced by his upbringing. This book is a testament to the authenticity and intricacies of life in this area, providing readers with a vivid and genuine portrayal of a misunderstood community.

Corey is proud alumnus of the University of Saint Mary and, honed his writing skills and knowledge to inspire and provoke thought. Residing in Southern California, he presents *South Central L. A. Divine Intervention* as a book and a gift to the world. Its a testament to his resilience, a man who has lived on the edge and returned to share his journey.